II. AUGUST III. FRIEDRICH CHRISTIAN. FR. AUGUS
3. 1733-1763. 1763. 1

Meissen's

Blue and White Porcelain

Dining in Royal Splendor

Nicholas Zumbulyadis

Schiffer Publishing Ltd

4880 Lower Valley Road, Atglen, PA 19310 USA

Other Schiffer Books on Related Subjects
The Book of Meissen, Robert E. Rontgen
Marks on German, Bohemian, and Austrian Porcelain 1710 to the Present, Robert E. Rontgen
Meissen Figures 1730-1775 The Kaendler Period, Yvonne Adams

Library of Congress Cataloging-in-Publication Data

Zumbulyadis, Nicholas.
Meissen's blue and white porcelain : dining in royal splendor / Nicholas Zumbulyadis.
p.cm.
Includes bibliographical references and index.
ISBN 0-7643-2482-9 (hardcover)
1. Meissen porcelain. 2. Ceramic tableware—Germany—History—18th century. 3. Ceramic tableware—Germany—History—19th century. 4. Blue and white ware—Germany—History—18th century. 5. Blue and white ware—Germany—History—19th century. I. Title.

NK4380.Z86 2006
728.2'7—dc22

2006014439

Designed by "Sue"
Type set in University Roman Bd BT/Lydian BT

ISBN: 0-7643-2482-9
Printed in China
1 2 3 4

Published by Schiffer Publishing Ltd.
4880 Lower Valley Road
Atglen, PA 19310
Phone: (610) 593-1777; Fax: (610) 593-2002
E-mail: Info@schifferbooks.com

For the largest selection of fine reference books on this and related subjects, please visit our web site at **www.schifferbooks.com**
We are always looking for people to write books on new and related subjects. If you have an idea for a book please contact us at the above address.

This book may be purchased from the publisher.
Include $3.95 for shipping.
Please try your bookstore first.
You may write for a free catalog.

In Europe, Schiffer books are distributed by
Bushwood Books
6 Marksbury Ave.
Kew Gardens
Surrey TW9 4JF England
Phone: 44 (0) 20 8392-8585; Fax: 44 (0) 20 8392-9876
E-mail: info@bushwoodbooks.co.uk
Website: www.bushwoodbooks.co.uk
Free postage in the U.K., Europe; air mail at cost.

Contents

Preface

Meissen's blue and white patterns are without a doubt the most popular patterns in the history of porcelain tableware. If collectibles can be defined as those treasured objects whose appeal has withstood the test of time, then the Blue Onion pattern certainly qualifies as the archetypal collectible.

The history of Meissen's blue and white patterns is the story of cross currents in the European decorative arts of the eighteenth century and their ultimate expression in nineteenth and twentieth century popular tastes. It is also the story of underglaze blue decorating technology, from its invention in the Middle East to its subsequent spread around the world, first from the Middle East to the Orient during the early Middle Ages and then from the Orient back to the West around the Renaissance. In this book I have attempted to capture this rich social, artistic, and technological history as much in pictures as in words.

Another objective of the book is to make the vast German literature and some original German sources on the subject of continental blue and white china accessible to English-speaking audiences.

The catalyst for my own personal interest in the subject has been the large and unique mid-nineteenth century Meissen Blue Onion dinner service that had descended through several generations of the Fosdick family before coming to our possession. It was the first major purchase of blue and white porcelain my wife and I made. The set has formed the nucleus of our own collection and has inspired and shaped its subsequent growth.

Throughout the writing of this book I have tried to keep in mind that it is a book intended primarily for collectors. With the possible exception of a handful of iconic objects from the Dresden Porcelain Collection, every piece depicted in this book is potentially obtainable by a determined collector. Most of the pictures do in fact originate from private collections. Whenever possible, price ranges are given in the figure captions. It would have been presumptuous and inappropriate, however, to assign specific values to items currently in museum collections. Nevertheless, auction outcomes for analogous, museum quality items from which values can be inferred are included in Appendix I.

The popularity of blue and white porcelain virtually assures that a book of this size on the subject cannot be complete. The cutoff date for the book's narrative is 1896, the year in which Julius Konrad Hentschel, one of Meissen's youngest and most promising modelers, won a prize with his design of the "Crocus

Dejeuner Service." This accomplishment signaled the dawn of the Art Nouveau period for Meissen and for the world of porcelain in general. All of the outstanding artistic achievements after that time including the Art Deco and post WW II periods were considered beyond the scope of the book. Even in the areas that I have chosen to cover in detail, the length of nearly every chapter could have easily been doubled.

I need to acknowledge the help and cooperation of numerous museums and passionate collectors. Without their goodwill the information presented in this book could not have been compiled.

My thanks go first and foremost to Prof. Dr. Bernhard von Barsewisch for his generous hospitality, sustained encouragement, and many valuable suggestions that have greatly contributed to this book. His extensive collection of eighteenth-twentieth century blue and white porcelain, the largest of its kind in the world, was the source of many photographs shown in the present work. The von Barsewisch Collection is on public display at the Schlossmuseum Wolfshagen, Prignitz, ancestral home of the Gans zu Putlitz family from which Dr. von Barsewisch is descended. The exhibit is a "must see" travel destination for every porcelain lover.

Thanks are due to the curators and staff of numerous museum collections. Karina Corrigan and Christine Michelini of the Peabody-Essex Museum in Salem, Massachusetts, Christina Green and Meredith Chilton of the Gardiner Museum in Toronto, Canada, Bonnie Lilienfeld and Ana Lopez of The Museum of American History, Division of Social History at the Smithsonian Institution, the staff of the Hetjens Museum in Düsseldorf, Germany, Stephanie Fawcett of the Victoria and Albert Museum, in London, England, Frau Yvonne Brandt and Frau Ulrike Maltschew of the Staatliche Kunstsammlungen in Dresden, Germany, Herr Uwe Beyer of the Staatliche Porzellanmanufaktur Meissen GmbH in Meissen, Germany, Dr. Verena Fink, Dr. Johanna Lessman, Herr Michael Unterberg and Herr Thomas Berg of the Museum für Kunst und Gewerbe in Hamburg, Germany, have all been very helpful in contributing many photographs and numerous suggestions to this project.

Thanks are due also to the auction house Bergmann of Erlangen, Germany, for making available images, detailed descriptions, and realized auction prices for many lots from their outstanding auctions. Their auction archives stretching back several years are readily available on line and represent an important resource as value guides to the European marketplace.

Last but not least, a word of deep gratitude is due to the owners of several significant private North American collections of blue and white porcelain for allowing me to take detailed photographs of their most prized possessions. The Doris P. Simonson Collection of nineteenth century Meissen Blue Onion tableware provided many of the rare figural pieces. Two other collectors from Upstate New York who wish to remain anonymous have also made very significant contributions to the present work. Both public and private sources for the images are acknowledged in the figure captions. Pictures without attribution are from my own collection.

Finally, I should be forgiven for starting the book with a somewhat technical chapter on the chemistry of porcelain and underglaze colors. I have spent my professional life as a research chemist and old habits are hard to break. But in a more serious vein, I strongly believe that an understanding of the composition and properties of this remarkable material we call porcelain, enhances our appreciation of the skill, inventiveness and hard work of generations of artisans who have transformed humble clay into the beautiful objects we admire and covet.

Ballade of Blue China
(ca. 1880)

There's a joy without canker or cark,
There's a pleasure eternally new,
'Tis to gloat on the glaze and the mark
Of china that's ancient and blue;
Unchipp'd all the centuries through
It has pass'd, since the chime of it rang,
And they fashion'd it, figure and hue,
In the reign of the Emperor Hwang.
Here's a pot with a cot in a park,
In a park where the peach-blossoms blew,
Where the lovers eloped in the dark,
Lived, died, and were changed into two
Bright birds that eternally flew
Through the boughs of the May, as they sang;
'Tis a tale was undoubtedly true
In the reign of the Emperor Hwang.

Andrew Lang (1844 - 1912)
Scottish poet, essayist, critic, and folklorist

PART I
Origins

Chapter I

The Chemistry and Technology of Porcelain and Porcelain Painting

First day cover and stamp commemorating the nominal 250th anniversary of the Blue Onion pattern. The year 1739 marks the beginning of large-scale production as the manufacturing process was sufficiently improved. The first documented examples of the pattern by Meissen date about a decade earlier.

The primary chemical elements that make up porcelain are also the three most common elements in the earth's crust, namely oxygen, silicon, and aluminum. Together they comprise over eighty percent of the world around us. Oxygen is the most abundant one. Silicon is the second most abundant element on earth after oxygen, making up about twenty-six percent of the earth's crust. In combination with oxygen and aluminum, silicon is the most significant structural material for the creation of human artifacts, from the crudest Neolithic pottery to the finest porcelain.

Three raw materials constitute the primary components of all true porcelain today; they are kaolin, quartz, and feldspar. Let us begin by understanding what these materials are, where they are found, and how they interact to form porcelain.

Kaolin is the clay used in porcelain making. Kaolin deposits form through the weathering of basaltic rocks and their primary constituent is a form of aluminum silicate with a layered structure at the molecular level. This form of aluminum silicate is known as kaolinite and has the chemical composition $Al_2[Si_2O_5](OH)_4$. Kaolinite is a mixed oxide of silicon and aluminum and because of the flat, two-dimensional structure of its molecules, it is known in chemistry as a layered silicate. The oxide layers can slip against each other and can also expand to accommodate water molecules between them. Changes in water content because of evaporation during firing lead to shrinkage and must be accounted for when molding pieces. The melting point of kaolinite is well above the temperature of the kilns used for making porcelain, and for this reason it is sometimes described as a "non-fusible" material. Besides kaolinite, kaolin as mined from the quarries may also contain variable amounts of quartz, feldspar, muscovite (a layered potassium alumosilicate), iron oxides, and traces of organic matter. The purity of kaolin varies depending on where it was mined, and its origin is very important in determining the quality and color tone of the resulting porcelain. Minor components can compromise the usability of the clay or the aesthetic appeal of the finished ware. Critical to the quality of the ensuing porcelain is the level (preferably total absence) of iron oxide.

Kaolin was used by the Chinese for the manufacture of clay articles since 200 A.D. and in fact its name probably derives from the Chinese word kao-lin meaning "high ridge" or alternatively from "Kao-ling" the name for a mountain where the first deposits were mined. The art of porcelain manufacturing spread from China to Korea, and was introduced to Japan around the year 1600 AD following Japan's Korean campaigns. It was in the years following that campaign that the legendary monk Ri Sampei discovered kaolin near the village of Arita on the Japanese island of Kyushu where a group of Korean artisans had been forcibly moved. Soon, the little village, about fifteen miles from the port of Imari, became the center of Japanese porcelain production.

Kaolin for the Meissen manufactory initially came from mines in Colditz. This material was high in iron and titanium oxide, giving rise to a rather yellowish product upon firing. This accounts for the light cream color of the earliest of Meissen porcelain The quality was improved by mixing the Colditz clay with clay from a mine in Aue near Schneeberg belonging to an ironsmith by the name of Schnorr, hence the name of the clay, Schnorr's earth or *Schnorrsche Erde*. Since 1764 kaolin from a mine in Seilitz, a village on the Elbe River, four to five miles downstream from Meissen, has been used. Today, a significant fraction of kaolin used for the manufacture of porcelain is industrially produced. According to Röntgen (Röntgen 1996), Meissen today uses an approximately 1:1 mixture of industrial Bohemian kaolinite and Seilitz kaolin.

The first attempts at making porcelain in the DuPaquier factory in Vienna by Christoph Conrad Hunger (a defector from Meissen) failed, in part because purportedly inferior kaolin from Passau was used. Another Meissen defector, Samuel Stöltzel successfully produced porcelain in Vienna using the kaolin from Aue, as in early Meissen. The kaolin for the first Berlin manufactory founded by Wilhelm Caspar Wegely in 1751 came from Hötensleben near Magdeburg. In 1765 the Royal Porcelain Manufactory (KPM), successor to the Wegely and Gotzkowsky companies, began using clay from the Zopten Mountains, near Tröbel in Silesia mixed with clay from Passau for making porcelain with warm yellowish tones. This was the best KPM porcelain ever made. In 1771 deposits of clay were discovered near Halle on the Saale River, and while this source was closer to the manufactory and thus more convenient and less expensive to transport, it resulted in KPM porcelain with a cold, blue tinged white tone. The kaolin clay for the French porcelain manufactories came from Saint-Yrieix, near Limoges where it was discovered in 1765. In 1769 Sèvres began producing hard-paste porcelain using kaolin from Limoges. The kaolin for the Danish Royal Copenhagen factory comes from the island of Bornholm, where it was first found in 1755. We will have more to say about the early history of the major porcelain manufactories of central Europe in later chapters.

The second component of porcelain after kaolin is quartz. Quartz is crystalline silicon dioxide. Unlike the layered structure of kaolinite, silicon and oxygen atoms in quartz are connected in the form of a three-dimensional rigid network that lacks plasticity, thus preventing excessive shrinkage during the firing of porcelain. Quartz occurs naturally also in kaolin deposits and may be present in sufficient quantities to obviate the need for further addition. According to Röntgen (Röntgen 1996) the Meissen Manufactory does not add any quartz into their formulations for porcelain paste.

Feldspar is a three-dimensional alumosilicate containing primarily potassium, and sometimes sodium or calcium. Its composition is given by $K[AlSi_3O_8]$. The function of feldspar is to act as a so-called flux. Feldspar softens and undergoes plastic flow at temperatures above 2100 ºF. As a fluid, it becomes a solvent for the other two constituents, which would otherwise not melt at the kiln temperature. Feldspar, too, is naturally present in kaolin clay.

The three constituents are separated from impurities as much as possible, milled into fine powders, and mixed in the right proportions in water to give a thick paste. The "right proportions" are a closely guarded trade secret and have also changed over time. The Chinese, who were the first to produce true porcelain accidentally, used clay that contained the three ingredients in roughly useable proportions. Later Chinese potters experimented with modifying the proportions of the various ingredients and came up with the optimal composition that suited their purposes.

Contemporary European hard paste porcelain uses compositions averaging 54% kaolin, 18% quartz, and 28% feldspar. The proportions of the three ingredients for the production of hard porcelain typical of Meissen are 67% kaolin, 8% quartz, and 25% feldspar (Sterba 1988). Soft porcelain (not to be confused with the so-called European soft-paste porcelain, which is not real porcelain at all, see Part I, Chapter II), similar to the original Chinese product, and produced in Europe most notably by the Sèvres factory in France, has a higher proportion of feldspar, consisting of 40% kaolin, 24% quartz, and 36% feldspar. Sèvres dropped its feldspar content with the introduction of *pâte nouvelle*. The typical modern utilitarian porcelain is also soft and is based on the Seger recipe after Hermann August Seger who was director of research at the Royal Porcelain Manufactory (KPM) in Berlin from 1878 until his retirement, and who compiled a series of standard porcelain formulas. Seger porcelain contains 25% kaolin, 45% quartz, and 30% feldspar and is reminiscent of Japanese formulations. High quartz content, also found in porcelain from the Nymphenburg Manufactory, makes porcelain more translucent but also renders it brittle and sensitive to sudden variations in temperature.

It is absolutely essential that the three components are mixed as homogeneously as possible. The quality of the porcelain depends critically on the mixing process. Once the powders of the three ingredients are thoroughly mixed, the water is extruded from the thick paste, and the resulting dough-like creamy yellowish mass is kneaded mechanically, shaped into large pancakes, and stored up to seven to ten months. Once properly aged, the pancakes are shaped into wonderful and utilitarian objects using essentially three techniques. Items with round contours like cups, vases, bowls, and plates are made by throwing the paste on the potter's wheel. Hollowware, figurines, odd-shaped cups or vases are made by first re-hydrating the paste to increase its fluidity and then pouring it into two-piece molds made of plaster of Paris. Relief ornamentation (more about it in later chapters) is also molded. Intricate decorations such as flowers, handles, and finials are carefully applied by hand. Latticework, as in the ever-popular reticulated Blue Onion plates, is also completed by hand at this stage of the manufacturing process by cutting out segments of the still very soft mass. This task requires a particularly skillful and steady hand, since the mass is hardly self-supporting.

At this point the object is ready for its first, low temperature firing, the so-called "glow-burning" (*Verglühbrand*) at 1500-1800ºF. During this firing the object undergoes significant changes in its physical properties, the most important being shrinkage, 16% in height and 14% in diameter. The material becomes porous and brittle. At this stage it is sometimes known as glowpaste porcelain. This is the term we shall use here following the convention set forth by G. Ware (Ware, 1946). The term bisquit is also used for this material. The term bisquit, however, is somewhat ambiguous, referring sometimes to a final product made of unglazed, undecorated, marble-like porcelain.

The first quality control step occurs after glow-burning. Pieces that have a distorted shape, or have developed firing cracks, or show dark specks of iron oxide occlusions are sorted out and eliminated. Also at this point in the manufacturing process the distinction between underglaze and overglaze decoration is made. If the piece is to receive the more common overglaze decoration, it is dipped in glaze and sent off to the "sharp firing" step (see below). If it is to receive underglaze decoration it is sent to the painting shop. Painting the decoration before the glazing process (underglaze decoration) has the obvious advantage that the painted pattern is enhanced in its durability because it is protected by the glaze from scratches, chipping off, and the like. Colors under the glaze appear more vivid and saturated. There are, however, also serious disadvantages and technical difficulties. The glowpaste object must have the exactly right degree of porosity to be acceptable for underglaze decoration. Porosity depends on the precise control of the glow-burning temperature. If the glow-burning has been too harsh, the resulting material is not porous enough to receive a sufficient amount of the colorant. If the temperature was not hot enough, the glowpaste is so porous that the decoration will bleed through to the underside or interior of the object. Only a few colorants are stable enough to survive the sharp firing step. This limits the color palette of the artist. Since glowpaste is porous and absorbent, any mistake during painting is irreversible and the piece must be discarded or relegated to a lower quality classification. Underglaze colorants if applied incorrectly will also cause glazing defects resulting in a product of unacceptable quality. That is why the first successful attempts at underglaze blue decoration in Meissen were not reported until 1720, a full ten years after the European invention of porcelain. We will have more to say about the history of this technology in the next chapter.

The underglaze colorants are typical metal salts that during the subsequent sharp firing step at 2550-2650°F will react with the aluminum oxide in the clay to form brightly colored metal aluminates.

The colorant for the underglaze blue decoration (contemporary technology since 1888) is a suspension of cobalt nitrate in a viscous, organic, carrier solvent such as glycerol, turpentine, or even sugar syrup. Cobalt nitrate has a deep purple-black color and the pattern as initially applied looks dark gray to black. A suspension of cobalt oxide particles in a similar carrier was used before 1888, a material known as smalt. Lazurite, also known as ultramarine or lapis lazuli, is a naturally occurring, blue-colored clay that owes its unusual color to a free radical of sulfur (the radical anion S_3^-). This material was considered during the early experiments in developing an underglaze blue colorant and was found to be unsuitable for this purpose. Other metal oxides used in this somewhat limited color palette include chromium oxide for green (introduced in 1817), iron oxide for brown and uranium oxide for black.

Today an underglaze pattern such as the Blue Onion is first roughly outlined on the unglazed surface by spraying charcoal black through a stencil, typically a metal foil or (in earlier times, see discussion of the SchulzCodex) a piece of drawing paper with holes. The stenciled outline is not very detailed, and individual "blue painters" like the one shown in Fig. 1 (more about the blue painters or *Blaumaler* in the following chapters) have the opportunity to express their individual manner of painting while still working within the canons of the pattern. The latitude the porcelain painters are given can be seen in a comparison of two contemporary demitasse saucers from the first quarter of the twentieth century shown in Fig. 2. The reader will immediately notice the minor differences between them.

Fig. 1. A blue painter at work in the Meissen Manufactory today. Note the outline of the pattern applied prior to painting and also the almost black color of the cobalt colorant prior to the sharp firing step (*reproduced with permission, Meissen GmbH, Meissen, Germany*).

Fig. 2. A pair of demitasse saucers (Meissen, c. 1888-1924), both decorated in the Blue Onion pattern, though contemporaneous, they differ in detail, (estimated value: $65-90 for a post-1888 cup and saucer).

Following the underglaze decoration, the glowpaste article is dipped by hand into the liquid glaze and completely covered by it. The decoration becomes temporarily invisible. The fluid glaze has essentially the same composition as the original paste with a little bit more feldspar added. Subsequently the items are placed in special fire resistant boxes (saggers) and subjected to the second or "sharp firing" (*Glattbrand* or *Scharffeuer*) at the high temperature of 2550 – 2650 °F. This is the step during which the marvelous chemistry takes place that transforms the humble glowpaste, hardly distinguishable in texture from common earthenware, to true porcelain fit for the tables of kings. The underglaze decoration miraculously reappears as it becomes visible again through the now vitrified glaze. The French Jesuit priest Père Francois Xavier d'Entrecolles (1664-1741), who as a missionary witnessed porcelain manufacturing in China in 1698, describes the process in a most poetic way in a letter written back home in 1712 (Burton, 1906):

> ...a beautiful blue colour reappears on porcelain after having been lost for some time. When the colour is first painted it is of a pale black; when it is dry and the glaze has been put upon it, it disappears entirely, and the porcelain seems quite white, the colour being buried under the glaze; but the fire makes it appear in all its beauty, almost in the same way as the natural heat of the sun makes the most beautiful butterflies, with all their tints, come out of their eggs.

The finished porcelain material consists of a vitreous (glassy) base with some of the aluminum silicate from the original kaolin crystallized out of the melt in the form of mullite, undissolved quartz, and air bubbles. The glassy base material is formed when feldspar softens at 2000-2200 °F and begins to dissolve first the kaolin and subsequently the quartz particles. Upon cooling, the base material solidifies into a translucent glass (vitrification) that imparts porcelain also its hardness and resonant ringing when lightly tapped. During sharp firing the underglaze colorants react with kaolin and are converted into their final color. Of interest to the subject matter of this book, cobalt nitrate reacts with kaolin to yield cobalt aluminate, $CoAl_2O_4$, known in chemistry as Thenard's Blue. At the same time, the underglaze decoration becomes visible again as the vitrified glaze in now transparent.

As many as two or more additional firing steps may be required before the final product is ready for the marketplace. One is associated with the overglaze decoration, which allows for a much broader range of colors and brings out the full potential of porcelain as the ideal canvas for painting. Porcelain allows, as no other medium does, the painting of crisp detail; the highly desirable KPM porcelain plaques, like the one shown in Fig. 3, being well-known examples.

Overglaze colorants are made by co-melting the inorganic, typically metal oxide pigment with glass powder in a 1:3 ratio, and regrinding the ensuing material, which is then suspended in syrup, turpentine, or a similarly viscous fluid to make the paint. Today, the palette of commercially available overglaze colors (also known as enamel colors) used in porcelain painting includes hundreds of colors. The Meissen Manufactory formulates its own colorants, numbering around 160, using closely guarded secret processes. Over fifteen different colors were already available to artists of the eighteenth century. The composition of the most important pigments used in early eighteenth century porcelain painting is given in the following table:

Fig. 3. Painting on porcelain (Royal Porcelain Manufactory Berlin, late 19th century), likely reproduction of an oil painting in overglaze colors on a porcelain plaque marked KPM impressed in verso, L 6.25", H 4.5", unsigned, (estimated value: $3,500-4,000).

Chemical Composition of the Major Pigments Used in eighteenth century Porcelain Painting

Color	Pigment Composition
Iron-red	Rust, iron oxide ore, oxidized iron, and steel filings
Yellow	Lead or antimony compounds
Green (leaves)	Oxidized copper or brass filings
Green (pastoral scenes)	Mixture of yellow and green pigments
Blue	Cobalt oxide, cobalt carbonate
Indian blue	Cobalt carbonate mixed with alkaline earth tartarates
Sea green	Indian blue and oxidized brass filings
Purple	Colloidal gold and stannous oxide
Brown	Umber
Japanese purple	Purple mixed with tartarate salts
Bluish-green	Cobalt carbonate mixed with oxidized copper or brass

The painted porcelain is fired a third time in a muffle furnace to about 1300-1450 °F. The enamel colors (or muffle furnace colors, *Muffelfarben*) fuse onto the glaze and become somewhat durable but can still be rubbed off after years of usage or if attacked by acids and other corrosive chemicals. A second technique of overglaze decoration involves using metal oxides that can endure high temperatures, like cobalt oxide, and subjecting the item to a second high temperature firing at around 1600 °F. This technique is used for the manufacture of porcelain with a uniformly deep cobalt blue (royal blue) and other ground colors, sometimes referred to as sharp fire colors (*Scharffeuerfarben*). During this process, the temperature is high enough that cobalt atoms actually migrate into and modify the atomic network of the alumosilicate glaze material. The incorporation of cobalt at the atomic level determines the rich dark hue of royal blue, and a sophisticated form of this manner of painting is sometimes referred to as inglaze painting for this reason. The discussion of overglaze color decoration is pertinent to our subject matter of underglaze blue decorated porcelain, because blue and white pieces have many times received additional polychrome decoration, either in the manufactories or from outside painters. We shall have more to say on this subject in later chapters.

An additional final firing step may be required when gilding is applied. The gilding of porcelain, with its roots in the decorative traditions of the late Baroque, represents a rather intricate manufacturing step, and it is the one decoration that is most easily lost to abrasion. The invention of a gilding formula that is at once durable and economical has been a century-long challenge for the Meissen manufactory. There are at least four approaches that were tried over the centuries, several of which are still in use. The earliest and costliest was of course the use of actual gold leaf, which was also not very durable. All other approaches are liquid-based and the gold decoration is applied by a painter's brush prior to firing.

The earlier technique is known as polished gilding (*Poliergold*). Typically fine gold powder, precipitated from a colloidal gold suspension is mixed with powdered bismuth(III) oxide (Bi_2O_3 reddish-brown) and lithium oxide (Li_2O) which serve as flux and very finely ground mercury oxide and/or charcoal black that serve as extenders. These ingredients are suspended in turpentine, syrup or some other viscous organic fluid to form a thick paste (gold paste) and painted on. After the application of the gold paste, the decorated item is fired just above 1500 °F, a temperature that is below the melting point of gold (1945.6 °F) but corresponds to the melting point of bismuth oxide (1515.2 °F). Gold films produced in this manner have a reddish hue and are dull in appearance. They need to be polished in special ways to attain either a matt or shiny surface. Most polished gilding techniques have their problems. The earlier ones required a lot of gold, about 40% - 60% of the formulation by weight. Later formulations allowed for the application of thinner layers, but these proved fragile and were not always robust enough to withstand the polishing step. Ways were invented to make them more robust but that required a separate firing step.

An acceptably durable gilding technique, that uses less gold, does not require a polishing step, and needs a comparatively low firing temperature of about 1100 °F was developed in 1827 by Heinrich Gottlob Kühn and is known as luster gilding (*Glanzgold*). It consists of organogold compounds dissolved in an organic solvent. During the firing step the organic part evaporates or decomposes, leaving behind a shiny thin film of metallic gold. This is the gilding technique in general use today.

A lost wax method is used for heavily gilt pieces. The areas to be gilded are covered by wax, which repels the glaze. The sharp firing step burns off the wax and the porous unglazed area becomes receptive to the gold preparation. After the subsequent firing, a rich and distinguished looking but lusterless gilding is obtained, known as gold bronze (*Goldbronze*). An example of gold bronze decoration on royal blue ground is shown in Fig. 4.

Fig. 4. Centerpiece bowl (Meissen, c. 1860), gold bronze accented foliage on royal blue ground, original gilding in mint condition, H 2.25", D 11" (estimated value: $400-500).

Besides underglaze and inglaze painting, the Meissen Manufactory experimented with a third way of producing blue and white decorated porcelain, namely transfer decoration. This method met with limited success. Very few such items are in production, mostly inexpensive collectibles like commemorative plates. All such items now carry the label Aquatinta. An example is given in Fig. 5.

Fig. 5. Charger (Meissen, 1980), transfer decorated pastoral scene, D 6" (estimated value: $60-70).

According to Röntgen (Röntgen 1996), demand for gilt porcelain slackened after 1855-60. The validity of this statement does not extend to blue and white tableware and certainly not to Blue Onion pieces, the most distinguished of which (as we shall see later) are still decorated with restrained and delicate gold trim.

A rare glimpse into the inner workings of a porcelain manufactory can be gotten in the series of photographs from the Saxonian Porcelain Manufactory Carl Thieme, now Dresden Porcelain, Inc. (*Sächsische Porzellanmanufaktur Carl Thieme*) shown in Figs. 6-9. The Thieme factory is the last remaining manufactory and decorating studio of Dresden's once flourishing porcelain industry. They produce decorative porcelain with overglaze polychrome handpainting of superior quality.

Fig. 6. A worker applying the finishing touches on what will eventually become a stunning figural candelabrum with putti (*amateur photograph, reproduced with permission, Dresden Porcelain, Inc., formerly Sächsische Porzellanmanufaktur Carl Thieme Dresden, Germany*).

Fig. 7. Bisquit porcelain objects waiting for the next step (*amateur photograph, reproduced with permission, Dresden Porcelain, Inc., formerly Sächsische Porzellanmanufaktur Carl Thieme Dresden, Germany*).

Fig. 8. Bisquit porcelain objects waiting for the next step (*amateur photograph, reproduced with permission, Dresden Porcelain, Inc., formerly Sächsische Porzellanmanufaktur Carl Thieme Dresden, Germany*).

Fig. 9. A vat of liquid glaze into which the bisquit object is dipped prior to the sharp firing step (*amateur photograph, reproduced with permission, Dresden Porcelain, Inc., formerly Sächsische Porzellanmanufaktur Carl Thieme Dresden, Germany*).

Thanks to its vitreous nature, the finished porcelain product has some remarkable properties that have made it a particularly desirable material for the production of tableware. Its nonporous surface is easy to keep clean; unlike earthenware or metal ware it does not impart an aftertaste to the food, it is strong and heat resistant, and its white color and translucency convey a sense of hygiene and wholesomeness. The appeal of porcelain is not just visual; it is also acoustic. Unlike pottery, which is polycrystalline at the microscopic level, in other words full of micro-cracks, the glassy nature of porcelain causes it to ring like a bell, and the higher its quality, the truer it rings. From the beginning, Meissen has taken great pride in its ability to produce porcelain with a pleasing ringing and showcases it in its products, like the elaborate dinner bell of Fig. 10

Fig. 10. Dinner bells (Meissen, 2000), six bells with underglaze blue decoration on a wooden mount. H 20.75" (estimated value $600-700).

Chapter II

The Decorative Impulses Leading to the Blue Onion and Related Blue and White Patterns on European Porcelain

We owe what finally became the most popular pattern in the history of porcelain tableware to the unique multicultural blending of European, Near Eastern, and Far Eastern decorative impulses. The origins of the Blue Onion and related patterns are to be found in the dining traditions of the Saxon court, in the preference for underglaze blue decoration rooted in the tastes of ancient Mesopotamia, and the fascination with Chinese and Japanese motifs in early German porcelain painting.

The Tradition of Elegant Dining at the Saxon Court

> In the middle of the Table was the Fountain...at least eight foot high, which ran all the while with Rose-water...
>
> From the observations of an Englishman dining with Count von Brühl (1748)

While the color of blue painted porcelain can be traced (as we shall see in the next section) to the Near East and many of its design motifs have been inspired by the Far East, the shapes are distinctly European. Blue Onion, and related pieces, were modeled by European artists and in their most popular forms they are extensions of Baroque and Rococo traditions.

For the ruling classes of the European monarchies, both great and small, the seventeenth and eighteenth centuries were a time of extravagance, conspicuous consumption, overwhelming decoration, and constant remodeling. Nowhere was that trend more evident than at the opulent banquets that accompanied every conceivable festive occasion, be it religious or secular. These banquets were intended to entertain several hundred guests at a time. They were designed by famous artists employed by the courts, and put in place by armies of artisans and handymen. Each banquet had its own theme, and was presented like the tableaux of a major theatrical production. Main courses, desserts, flower bouquets, statuary, and decorations were all arranged in harmony to reflect the spirit of the occasion.

The aristocrats and influential elites of the eighteenth century had a solid schooling in classical literature and mythology, philosophy, and history. They preferred to communicate in implicit terms with a penchant for cultural allusions, and allegory. This tendency was evident also in the decorative arts of the period where form and design often stood symbolically for universal themes and veiled messages. Continents, the seasons, the senses were all represented by shapes. An Indian on an alligator for example would stand for America, sheaves of wheat for summer, or a lady at the table for taste. Even abstract notions such war and peace, victory and defeat, joy and sorrow, love and marriage, faithfulness and betrayal, all had their respective icons that were weaved together to tell a story. Allegories were a means of subtle and sophisticated communication. This passion for symbolic representation also dominated banquet decorations.

In the German Empire, Saxony with Dresden as its capital was becoming the center of culture and artistic sophistication. By that time the House of Wettin had ruled over the lands of eastern Germany bounded by the Neisse, Elbe, and Werra rivers for almost 600 years. Its founder, Konrad the Great (1098-1157), was Margrave of Meissen 1123-1156. A margravate (*Markgrafschaft*) referred to an earldom (the lands of a count) at the eastern borderlands (the Marches) of the German Empire. Following the Division of Leipzig in 1485, the House of Wettin split into two lineages. The Albertine lineage chose Dresden as its city of residence. The city's twelfth century fort was converted into a royal palace (*Residenzschloß*) in 1503-1537. It was further expanded in the Renaissance style by Duke Moritz in 1547, when the title of Prince Elector was conferred upon the Albertine line.

Following the devastations of the Thirty Year War the Wettiners, starting with Prince Elector Johann Georg II, rebuilt Saxony and made Dresden a center of culture and the arts rivaling Paris and Versailles in grandeur. Courtly splendor became particularly extravagant under August the Strong (1670-1733), Prince-Elector of Saxony and later also King of Poland. The standard was set by the grand scale of festivities at the court of Louis XIV at Versailles, which August sought to emulate. During his reign, major banquets became occasions for artistic expression in architecture, poetry, music, and theater.

Of central importance in these activities were the creations of the royal confectioner (*Hofkonditor*). These creations included figurines, flowers, trees, and animals, as well as architectural models of mythological temples, real palaces, arcades, and promenades, even cities. The individual creations would be assembled into groupings that told a story or carried a symbolic message appropriate for the occasion. The confectioners worked literally as sculptors, modeling the individual pieces by hand out of a white edible plastic material that consisted of powdered sugar mixed with a gum known as tragacanth. Tragacanth was extracted from the stems of astragalus, a spiny leguminous plant that grows in Anatolia and the Near East. The most desirable varieties of tragacanth came from Smyrna, Syria, and Persia.

Johann Ulrich König, master of ceremonies at the Saxon court, chronicles the wedding of Maria Amalia, daughter of King August III, to King Charles IV of the House of Bourbon, (the later King Charles III of Spain) in May 1738. In his diary König describes with great reverence the work of the royal confectioner, *Herr Cortier*. According to König, on May 9, the first evening of the ceremonies, the theme was Love and Devotion. The centerpiece was a temple with a reticulated cupola on classic columns and a flight of stair leading to its entrance. The cupola was colored sky-blue and further had red applied decorations. The columns were yellow, resting on red pedestals. On either side of the temple were pairs of white intertwined hearts resting on four-inch tall glass supports and decorated with pink bows and arrows. On the second evening of the banquet, the guests were treated to a scaled model of the Bay of Naples, including its famous lighthouse, all made of sugar and tragacanth paste.

These were of course ephemeral creations that spoiled soon after they were made and had to be recreated on every occasion. Records show that in 1753 the Prince-Electoral Court Confectionary in Dresden employed thirty-five artisans. The modeling of the tragacanth paste, the application of smaller pieces onto larger ones, the drying and the subsequent painting of the objects are all procedures remarkably analogous to the steps involved in making porcelain objects. Not surprisingly, the art of the confectioners of the late Baroque and ascending Rococo periods has had a great impact on the evolution of European porcelain tableware. Porcelain had the added advantage of durability; it could be reused. Just as some of the most talented court artists participated in the creation of sugar paste sculptures, confectioners were part of the design team for the grandest dinner service ever made by Meissen, the dinner set for Heinrich Count von Brühl in the 1730s.

Nothing illustrates this trend more vividly than the monumental porcelain centerpiece shown in Fig. 11 created for a banquet hosted by Prince Elector Friedrich August II (as King, August III), son of August the Strong. The banquet was held on March 5, 1749. The famous porcelain modeler Johann Joachim Kaendler (more about him in a later chapter) toiled for two years on its design and firing. The centerpiece known as the "Great Temple of Honor" (*großer Ehrentempel*) was over 10 ft (3.56 m) tall. The original was auctioned off in 1778 for 5,000 Thalers. A later pull of it produced in 1920-30 in celebration of the 200th birthday of August the Strong can be seen today at the museum of the Meissen Manufactory.

Fig. 11. Monumental centerpiece (Meissen, c. 1747-48) this pull originates from c. 1920-30 (*amateur photograph, reproduced with permission, Meissen GmbH, Meissen, Germany*).

An entry in the "*Frauenzimmer-Lexicon*" (*Dictionary for the Lady of the House*) of 1773, already points out that porcelain statuary for the table from the Meissen, Berlin, and Vienna factories reduces greatly the workload of the confectioners. And in a 1774 handbook of the trades and arts ("*Handwerke und Künste in Tabellen*" by P. N. Sprengel) the confectioner of the previous century is presented as an almost accomplished sculptor, whose art, however, is now being gradually displaced by porcelain. The consequence of this disruptive new technology was that elegant banquets could now be arranged without recourse to an army of confectioners. Elegance was finally within the reach not just of royalty but also of the upper class of the times, i.e. wealthy merchants, leading bankers, and high-ranking civil servants.

As the upper middle class began emulating the ways of the royalty, the dressing out of eighteenth century banquet tables was standardized in good housekeeping books and desserts assumed a special place. They were the crowning conclusion of a sumptuous dinner and until served they would be on display. It was only natural therefore that their containers, like tureens, sweetmeat dishes, centerpieces, and etageres would be considered "Regalia for the Sideboard" (an expression I borrow from McKearin 1955). As will be described in greater detail in a later chapter, some of the more elaborate nineteenth century blue and white figural porcelain dinnerware with all its amorous innuendos, often described as statuary for the dinner table, has its origins in this custom. Meissen pieces of the twentieth century continue to reflect this tradition.

Centuries later Meissen paid proper homage to the Wettiner Dynasty and the tradition of glorious dining they ushered into the royal courts, mansions, and villas of the wealthy of Central Europe. The history of the House of Wettin is commemorated on a massive mural on the wall of the royal palace in Dresden, a stunning example of Meissen's public art. It consists of 25,000 tiles with underglaze painting depicting the entire lineage of the House of Wettin marching in procession. This masterpiece, that has endured harsh winters and survived the Allied bombing of Dresden, was manufactured by Meissen during 1905-06 and erected in 1907. It replaced the similar mural from 1876 in the sgrafitto technique by Wilhelm Walther that had succumbed to weathering. The section of the mural depicted in Fig. 12 shows Prince Elector Friedrich the Gentle (*Sanftmütige*) and his two sons Ernst and Albrecht the Brave. After Friedrich's death the two sons governed the lands of the margravate jointly until the aforementioned Division of 1485. The castle that ultimately became the site of the Meissen Manufactory was built during Albrecht's reign and later named after him.

Fig. 12. Detail from the Meissen mural "The Procession of the House of Wettin." Elector Friedrich the Gentle (*Sanftmütige*) and his two sons, Ernst and Albrecht the Brave, builder of the Albrechtsburg, which almost 250 years later became the site of the Meissen Porcelain Manufactory.

Fig. 13. Detail from the Meissen mural "The Procession of the House of Wettin." August the Strong depicted on rearing horse in contrast to all the other princes.

The Fascination with Underglaze Blue Decoration

"Like the blue of a delightful summer night"

from a Chinese poetic description of the underglaze blue porcelain made in Jingdezhen

Scholars are not in agreement on whether the glazing of earthenware was first invented in Egypt or Mesopotamia. Vividly colored tiles and bricks occurring at both places date roughly to the same period. A dark blue glaze was in use in Egypt during the VI Dynasty (2550-2350 BC). The tin-based glazes we shall later encounter in conjunction with Italian maiolica and Delft pottery were already in use on tiles and bricks in Nineveh around 500 BC and were rediscovered by Arab potters. As the people of the Near East mastered tin-glazing, they also developed the art of painting with brilliant underglaze blue colors. The blue color was derived from cobalt oxide mined in the hills near Kashan. Kashan, situated in today's Iran, halfway between Teheran and Isfahan, was for a long time a prominent center of Islamic pottery. Blue decorated pottery from this region dates back to the ninth century AD. The striking underglaze blue color of Islamic pottery soon became known among Chinese and Europeans as "Mohammedan Blue." These wares were, however, pottery not porcelain.

As we briefly mentioned in Chapter I, the Chinese were the first to accidentally fire a clay mixture containing kaolin and create the earliest known porcelaneous material around 200 AD. Vessels made from such material and dating to the Han Dynasty (206 BC - 220 AD) can be seen at the Field Museum in Chicago. Their hardness and the presence of kaolinite identify them as porcelaneous, their appearance, color, and glazing technique, however, are still rather crude. Over the centuries Chinese potters refined and perfected their techniques until, during the T'ang Dynasty (618-906 AD), the first true porcelain was made, which in the words of W. B. Honey (Honey 1962) "aroused unbounded admiration and wonder" to wherever it was exported. Great quantities of it were exported to Persia and to the Arab Middle East. They reached Western Asia initially by the overland routes established already since the time of Alexander the Great and used by the Romans for the silk trade. Since the thirteenth century the trade was carried out also via Arab and Chinese junks that plowed the waters of the Indian Ocean, the Persian Gulf, and the Red Sea. Archeological excavations that are very significant to the history of porcelain have been carried out at the palace of the Abbasid Caliph Matasim in Samarra on the Tigris River in today's Iraq. These excavations have turned out Chinese porcelain as well as pottery fragments by indigenous and Chinese artisans. Since the palace is known to have been occupied relatively briefly, 836-883 AD, the porcelain is clearly of T'ang origin.

The potters of Kashan tried hard to reproduce this enchanting material. An analysis of the chemical composition of porcelain in the modern sense was, of course, not possible at the time. To an observer, the most distinctive feature of porcelain is its translucency. In trying to emulate this aspect of porcelain, the Kashani potters invented an artificial kind of porcelain known as fritware. It was made of ten parts ground silica, one part glass, and one part of clay. The mixture was heated only to the melting temperature of glass and the resulting translucent material bore a superficial resemblance to porcelain, but lacked its mechanical hardness and heat resistance. A major center for the production of underglaze blue decorated fritware was the Ottoman Turkish town of Iznik. During the sixteenth century, Iznik wares were imported to Continental Europe and the British Isles in large quantities.

Artistic influences flowed West-to-East as well as East-to-West. The shapes of T'ang Dynasty ewers, for example, show distinct classical Greek as well as later, Islamic influences. This influence on shapes did not extend initially to the taste for the color of glazes. The "Mohammedan blue" that started out in Persia and spread throughout the Moslem Near East had at first little impact on the Chinese taste. The Chinese showed a distinct preference for the delicate turquoise glaze, known to us as celadon, until the end of the Song dynasty (960-1280 AD).

Some Chinese researchers date the Far Eastern beginnings of porcelain painting in underglaze cobalt blue tones to the Song dynasty, but most scholars today agree that it probably began during the Yuan dynasty (1280-1368 AD) that reigned during the Mongol occupation. The Mongols conquered northern China in 1280 and the last Song emperor committed suicide by casting himself into the sea. Genghis Khan's grandson Kublai took charge of China, establishing the Yuan dynasty. His nephew Hulagu had already conquered Baghdad in 1258. A trans-Asiatic Mongol empire was taking shape. Kublai and his successors secured the trade routes to the Middle East. Muslims in great numbers began arriving in China, and the Arabs even conquered parts of Sumatra. The Mongol invasion of Southern China in 1322-1330 had a profound cultural effect on many aspects of Chinese civilization, the art of porcelain decoration being among them. With the influx of Moslems and the securing of the caravan routes, the "Mohammedan blue" found its way across the trans-Asiatic Mongol empire from the Middle East to the Far East and the blue and white decorative elements on pottery and porcelain were introduced.

During the Song dynasty the kilns of Jingdezhen, established in the twelfth century, had risen to prominence as centers of porcelain, producing celadon glazed wares that suited the refined Chinese tastes of the period. During the period of the Yuan dynasty, Jingdezhen began producing cobalt blue underglaze ware. This was an absolutely amazing technical accomplishment given the difficulties Meissen encountered centuries later in mastering the underglaze blue color on porcelain. These wares were exported back to the Middle East and Seljuk-Turkish dominated Asia Minor but they were initially dismissed as crude and vulgar by the Chinese themselves. When the Mongol Yuan dynasty was overthrown in 1368, the succeeding Chinese national Ming dynasty (1368-1664), after a brief interruption, resumed trade first with the Middle East and subsequently with the Ottoman Turks, and through them and the Portuguese and later Dutch sea merchants, with Western Europe.

The first specimens of Chinese porcelain in Europe arrived in Venice in 1295 with the return of Marco Polo from his legendary travels through the Far East. Trade between the Italian city-states and the Middle East in the fifteenth century introduced blue decoration to Southern Europe. The discovery of the sealanes from Europe to Asia expanded trade in the sixteenth century. First the Portuguese, then the Dutch, and finally the English gained control of the porcelain trade with the Far East. During the mid-sixteenth century the Portuguese merchant-sailor Antonio Peixoto and his partners Antonio da Mota and Francisco Zeimoto traveled around the Chinese coast in a barge loaded with hides and other European commodities. They traded their wares for porcelain in the port of Quanzhou, though they were not allowed to go ashore. The trade journey is documented by two porcelain ewers (one at the Victoria and Albert Museum in London and shown in Fig. 14) dating to the reign of the Ming emperor Jiajing (1522-1566) that bear the coat of arms of the Peixoto family in blue underglaze decoration.

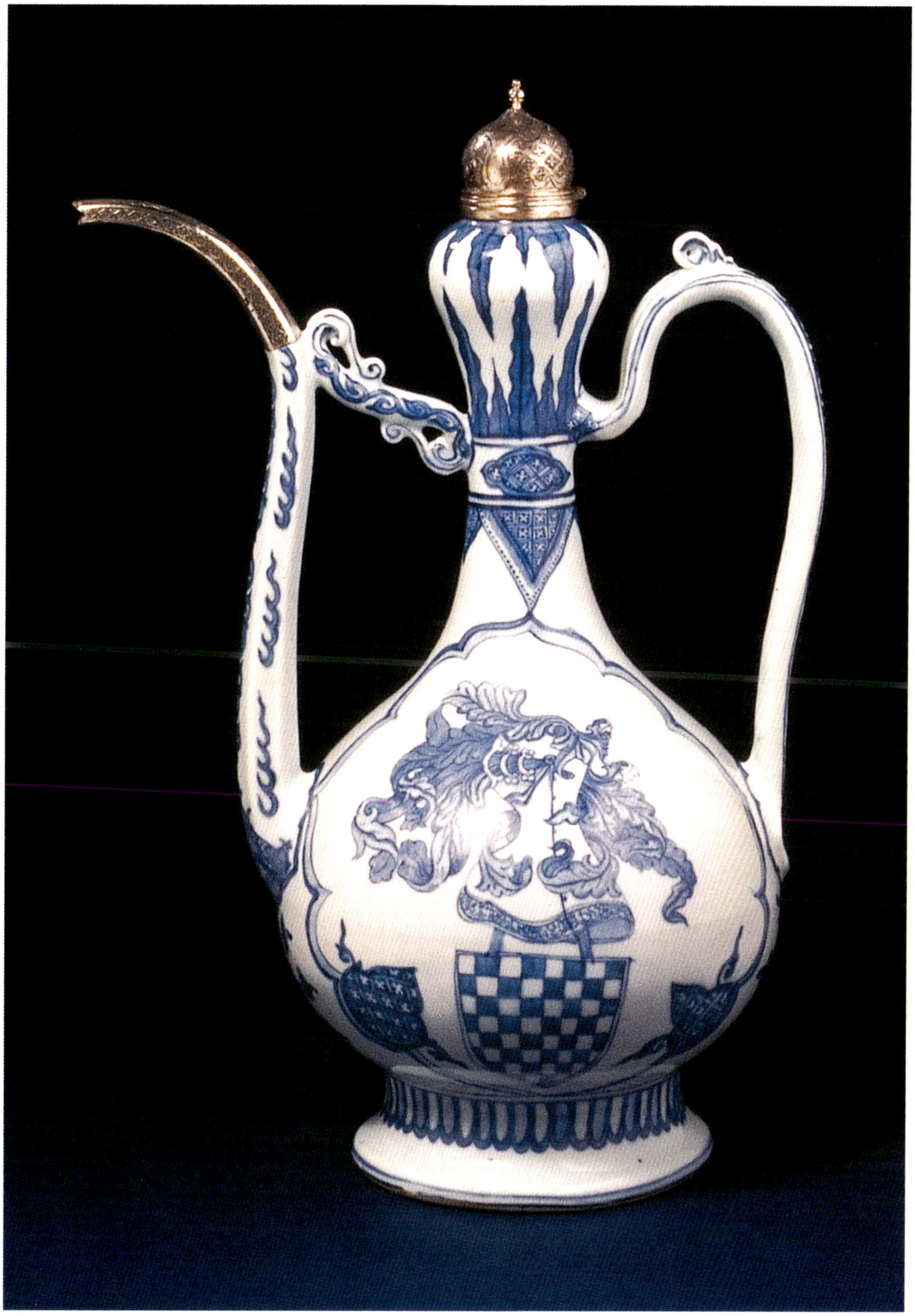

Fig. 14. Ewer with Persian silver mounts (Chinese, Jiajing Period, 1522-1566). Porcelain with underglaze blue decoration, depicting probably the coat of arms of the Peixoto family. H 13.25" *(reproduced with permission, V&A Images/The Victoria and Albert Museum, London).*

To appreciate the esteem in which Chinese blue and white porcelain was held one needs only to examine how it was further embellished by Middle Eastern and European craftsmen. The Peixoto ewers are further enhanced with almost contemporaneous Persian silver mounts. Another example cited by Honey in this context (Honey 1962) is a Chinese blue-and-white bowl at the Metropolitan Museum of Art. Dating from the period of Ming emperor Wan Li (1573-1619), it is richly decorated with intricate metal mounts of European origin. The Portuguese imports of Chinese blue and white porcelain also gained popularity in Holland where they were known as *kraak*, a term derived from the word *caracca*, a type of Portuguese ship used in the East India trade. After 1600 the Dutch established a more regular China trade of their own. Much of the blue-and-white porcelain imported by the Dutch East India Company was brought to London to be given elaborate gilt silver mounts.

An example closer to home for the American collector can be seen in the Asian export porcelain collection of the Peabody-Essex Museum, in Salem and is shown in Figs. 15 and 16. It is a large charger from the reign of emperor Jiajing. The charger is decorated in underglaze blue, and as currently displayed also has as embellishments ormolu mounts and overglaze gilding of the blue foliate pattern. According to curator Karina Corrigan, the charger had no embellishments when it arrived in Europe in the late 1600s. The mounts are of German origin and were added about the time of its arrival in Europe. The gilding was added even later, around 1720. This presages the practice of overdecoration applied afterwards by outside painters that we shall discuss in greater detail in a later chapter.

Fig. 15. Porcelain charger (China, c. 1522-66) with gilt bronze mounts of European, likely German, origin from the late 17th century, and even later gold highlighting of the underglaze blue pattern from c. 1720 (*reproduced with permission, Peabody Essex Museum, Salem MA*).

Fig. 16. Side view of the charger shown in Fig. 015 (*reproduced with permission, Peabody Essex Museum, Salem MA*).

Fig. 17. Tin glazed earthenware charger of North African origin decorated with Hispano-Moresque motifs in underglaze cobalt blue and other colors, (possibly Moroccan, latter half of the 19th century), D 14", H 3" (estimated value $250-275).

Thus fascination with blue and white decoration began to spread throughout the continent. High-temperature cobalt-blue decorations inspired by Middle Eastern and Far Eastern originals became fashionable on the earthenware of fifteenth, sixteenth, and seventeenth century Europe. At the beginning of the fifteenth century Florence, then an independent Italian city-state, had emerged as the dominant commercial and naval power of its time. Florentine traders returning from their trade journeys through Egypt, Syria, and Persia imported blue decorated porcelain of Chinese origin and thirteenth century blue Egypto-Syrian earthenware to Italy. A so-called "Impasto blue Florentine ware" was developed that quickly replaced the "Green Florentine ware" developed by the potters of Florence at the beginning of the Renaissance. They mastered the technique of using tin glaze. Tin glaze, introduced to Europe by the Moorish potters of South Spain, could be applied evenly and gave a white surface that could be decorated with blue pigments. This tin-glazed earthenware became known as Italian maiolica. With the rise of Spanish power, the Middle Eastern décor on these blue wares was replaced by the Hispano-Moresque motifs of North African origin. An example of this style of decoration is the charger shown in Fig. 17

Parallel to the developments in Florence, blue earthenware were gaining popularity elsewhere in Italy, most notably in Faenza, Siena, Venice, Padova, Urbino (the birthplace of Raphael), and Castel Durante. Of these, Faenza has given us the term "faience", officially accepted as a word into the French language in 1574.

Blue decorated European soft paste porcelain, known as Medici porcelain, also falls into this period. Grand Duke Francesco Maria Medici, himself trained as an alchemist, working together with Bernardo Buontalenti and Oratio Fontana and "with the assistance of a Levantine," meaning most likely a Persian, made the first so-called European soft paste porcelain in 1575 (Wynter 1972). It was made from kaolin-containing clay from Vicenza mixed with ground glass but no feldspar and fired at a very low temperature, just enough to melt the glass and give the ensuing material a translucency like porcelain. In this respect Medici pseudo-porcelain is very reminiscent of Kashani fritware, and probably reflects "the assistance of a Levantine" mentioned in the chronicles. The yellowish material was glazed with tin to make it white and painted in cobalt blue or manganese violet tones. The painting was covered with a second transparent lead glaze. Medici pseudo-porcelain was made in Florence until 1586 and production was continued in Pisa until 1620. Only thirty highly coveted pieces of Medici porcelain survive in museums today, in the Louvre in Paris, at the Musee National de Ceramique in Sèvres, and at the Victoria and Albert Museum in London. Variants of this material that did not contain kaolin were also produced widely in France most notably in St Cloud, Rouen, and Chantilly. European soft-paste is, as the name implies, very soft, and unlike true hard porcelain, it can be easily scratched with a steel blade (hence the French word *pate tendre*)

The blue cobalt pigment of the Italian wares, called "Zaffara", was imported first from the Middle East and since the 1500s from Schneeberg, near Aue, in the Erzgebirge region of Germany along the border with today's Czech Republic, a location we have already encountered in conjunction with our discussion of porcelain technology.

One way that blue decorated wares found their way to central Europe was indeed through Venice. Armorial plates originating from Venetian kilns made for the patrician families of southern Germany and bearing their coat-of-arms can be seen in various European museums, primarily in London, Berlin, Dresden, Hamburg, Leipzig, and Nuernberg, today.

The familiar Dutch blue decorated tin glazed pottery is also of Italian origin. In 1548 Guido di Savino set up shop in Antwerp, in today's Belgium, spreading the art of maiolica potting. In 1560-70 Antwerp potters were forced to flee as protestant refugees to the Northern provinces (areas that later became Holland). The cities of Rotterdam and Haarlem briefly rose to prominence as centers of tin-glazed earthenware. By around 1650, however, Delft became the preeminent center for the production of pottery that was exported throughout Europe. Records indicate that already during the mid-sixteenth century Dutch merchants, too, traveled to Schneeberg to obtain cobalt ore. In 1609 alone, as the records show, they paid the prince-elector of Saxony mining taxes for 400 metric tons (4000 *Zentner* or hundredweight). The pigments were sold to Delft potters but were also exported to Spain, England, even China. The Dutch potters went so far as to coin the name "*Delfsche porseleyn*" even though Delftware like the Medici porcelain and other European soft paste porcelain is not of porcelaneous nature at all!

The Dutch gained familiarity with Chinese porcelain primarily through the imports of the Dutch East India Company, which was founded in 1602. The Company had 150 merchant ships, 40 war ships, and through 10,000 mercenaries controlled eight governments from the Persian Gulf to Ceylon and the Straits of Malacca. Although huge amounts of Chinese porcelain were imported to Europe, the Dutch East India Company had limited contact with China. Chinese decoration brought to Holland was consequently never fully understood, merely copied. Delft pottery came very close in appearance to Chinese porcelain, and also benefited economically from the interruption of the Chinese trade, following the fall of the Ming dynasty, for forty years after 1634 when the last vessel with 400,000 pieces of Chinese porcelain sailed into Dutch waters.

Joan Nieuhof had traveled with the first delegation of the East India Company to China (1655-1657) and drew extensive sketches of his travels during 1656. His drawings visually captured the nature, architecture, and customs of these lands as he perceived them, though he did not understand their origin and meaning. Two other trips by Dutch delegations followed. The sketches of Far Eastern life accumulated throughout the seventeenth century and were published as copper engravings during the first two decades of the eighteenth century. As we shall see later, these engravings were acquired relatively early by the Meissen Manufactory to be used as models.

The pottery painters (*plateelschilders*) of Delft embraced a variety of Chinese underglaze blue decorative elements, particularly stylized peonies, lotus blossoms, and chrysanthemums, as well as leaves, twigs, and branches. Another recurring decorative element was the peacock, a bird native to East Asia. These elements found one of their finest expressions in the Lobkowic dinner service made around 1670 for Count Ferdinand Wenceslas Lobkowic by the *De Metalen Pot* factory under the direction of Lambert Cleffius (Warren 1982). The basic constituent pieces of the service as they survive today include plates, cups and saucers, and dishes of various sizes, but also an ewer, candlesticks, variedly shaped sweetmeat dishes, wine coolers, an octagonal sugar shaker, a tea caddy, and salt cellars. The remarkable diversity of the Lobkowic service presages in some way that of the later Meissen services. The fascination of the Delft factories with underglaze blue decoration was also expressed by decorative elements that were not Oriental but Mediterranean in origin. An example would be the dinner service in the ownership of the Harrach family (made originally for Count Ferdinand Bonaventura von Harrach zu Rohrau) by *De Grieksche* A factory under Adriaen Kocks (and later his son and his widow) around 1701-22. This service also displays a diversity of form; however both the decoration (heavy on putti) and the shapes derive from Italian maiolica. Delft services lost their desirability after 1720, as – thanks to renewed trade ties with China after the re-establishment of the kilns at Jingdezheng by the emperor Kangxi – the volume of imported Oriental porcelain, as well as European production volumes, increased dramatically. The nobility and ruling classes of Central Europe that always clearly favored porcelain could now obtain it readily and in large quantities. Just as the faience factories of Delft imitated Chinese porcelain designs on pottery, so did the Chinese reproduce, in porcelain, forms and underglaze blue decorations that were purely European in origin. Two significant examples from the Victoria and Albert Museum in London, a coffeepot and a tulip vase, are shown in Fig. 18.

Fig. 18. (*left*) Tulip vase (Chinese, c. 1700): Porcelain with underglaze blue decoration possibly a copy of a Delft pottery design by Adriaen Kocks (De Grieksche A). H 14.5"; (*right*) Coffee pot (Chinese, c. 1700-1720): Porcelain with underglaze blue decoration, possibly a copy of a Delft pottery design by Lambert van Eenhoorn (*De Metalen Pot*). H 11.75" (*reproduced with permission, V&A Images/The Victoria and Albert Museum*).

The Popularity of Far Eastern Motifs in the Decoration of German Porcelain

"We fetch our models from the wise Chinese."

Of Taste: An Essay by James Cawthorn 1756

As we have already seen, Chinese decorative elements played a great role in the decoration of European tin-glazed earthenware and soft-paste porcelain since the sixteenth century. European nobility during these times also possessed genuine Chinese porcelain, such as boxes and vases, albeit in small quantities. Antoine Lebel (Lebel 2005) describes the holdings of the French royal family. His examples include about three pieces in the possession of King Francis I (ca. 1547) and forty-two pieces belonging to one of his ministers. The French Royal family became avid collectors of Chinese blue and white porcelain with the ascendancy to the throne of the *Roi soleil* (Sun King), Louis XIV, in 1643. His brother Philippe had an extensive collection of blue decorated Chinese porcelain at the Château de Saint-Cloud. Louis XIV's own inventory included over eight hundred pieces of Chinese porcelain, many of them blue decorated. In 1695 he gave his son Louis, the Grand Dauphin, the Château de Meudon, where two rooms were dedicated to underglaze blue Chinese porcelain, most of it with European ormolu (gilt bronze) mounts.

True to the Wettiner ambition to make Dresden a center of culture, style, and fashion, August the Strong was determined to compete with *le Roi soleil*. The collection of Chinese porcelain was one of the areas of competition. In fact in later years August described his addiction to porcelain as having succumbed to the "porcelain sickness" (*maladie de porcelain*). The famous "Dragoon Vases" incident palpably demonstrates, perhaps as no other, his compulsive desire for Chinese porcelain in underglaze blue. Friedrich Wilhelm I, King of Prussia, had inherited two palaces (Charlottenburg and Oranienburg) full of porcelain from his father, King Friedrich I. He did not however inherit the latter's passion for porcelain. Wilhelm was thrifty and much more inclined to build up Prussia's military might. The proceeds from the sale of his father's art treasures went toward strengthening the Prussian war machine, earning him the nickname the soldier-king (*Soldatenkönig*). August became intensely interested in this collection of porcelain and in 1715 initiated negotiations for its acquisition. The two monarchs reached an agreement in 1717 whereby 151 pieces of Oriental porcelain would be exchanged for 600 mounted and fully equipped Saxon dragoons and their horses. Among the many pieces were several monumental underglaze blue decorated vases of the Kangxi period. They became known as the Dragoon vases (*Dragonervasen*) and can be seen at the Dresden Porcelain collection. Just a few months later the first successful piece of blue and white porcelain came out of the Meissen kilns. But, as we shall describe in greater detail in the next chapter, this was not yet a consistently reproducible accomplishment.

August's lavish spending on fashion and style had begun putting pressure on the state treasury from the beginning of his reign. In fact, it could be argued that his profligacy catalyzed the European invention of porcelain. (The reader is referred to "*The Arcanum*" by Janet Gleeson for a most entertaining history of the discovery of European porcelain.) August needed gold and he needed it fast, so enter the character of Johann Friedrich Böttger (Fig. 19).

Fig. 19. Engraving of Johann Friedrich Böttger, also showing his signature and title of "Administrator."

Böttger was born on February 4, 1682, in Schleiz. His stepfather, a military engineer, insured his thorough schooling. At the age of fourteen Böttger came to Berlin to begin his training as an apprentice to the pharmacist Friedrich Zorn. While diligent as an apprentice, and carefully following established rules for turning out pills and ointments, Böttger also felt the need for an exciting and creative outlet and developed an interest in alchemy. In a 1697 letter to his mother when he was barely seventeen years old he claimed to having been successful in his attempts at transmutation (a chemically impossible process that purports to transform base metals into gold) and promised to make her rich beyond belief. When challenged by Zorn in 1701 he gave a public demonstration of his alleged gold maker skills, a demonstration so convincing that even Gottfried Wilhelm Leibniz, the great scholar and mathematician of that time, found it hard to refute the many eyewitness accounts. King Friedrich I of Prussia became intensely interested in this work and ordered that Böttger be brought to him at once.

Fig. 20. The Dresden casemates today as seen from the outside; located under Brühl's Terrace, they are the last remaining vestige of the city fortification.

Böttger knew what this meant. He either had to deliver the gold or face the gallows. He escaped over the border to the Saxon city of Wittenberg, where August the Strong took him into protective custody and brought him to Dresden. Böttger was given space in an old laboratory and asked to perfect his process of transmutation.

In 1702 Böttger met the eminent physicist and engineer Ehrenfried Walther von Tschirnhaus, who was interested in the chemical transformations minerals undergo when exposed to high temperatures. He was a pioneer in the use of giant polished copper mirrors and large specialty lenses to generate record high temperatures for his day and age. He demonstrated that some minerals could be molten under these conditions, just like metals. He was the first to melt complex magnesium and calcium silicates. Tschirnhaus had purely practical and utilitarian objectives in mind. These objectives had led him in 1700 to begin scientifically systematic inquiries into the nature of porcelain. He is credited with the key observation that certain additives like gypsum, calcium carbonate or feldspar can be used as fluxes to facilitate the melting of minerals like kaolin. As we saw in the first chapter on the chemistry and technology of porcelain, the use of fluxes is the key enabling step in porcelain manufacture.

In 1705 Böttger was moved to the Albrechtsburg in Meissen and given five assistants versed in metallurgy and mineralogy, among them two who were destined to play pivotal roles in the future development of porcelain technology, Johann David Köhler and Samuel Stöltzel. In 1706, during the Swedish occupation of Dresden, Böttger had to interrupt his work while he was brought to safety in the fortress of Königstein. When the Swedes vacated Dresden in 1707 he was given a new laboratory in the Bastion of the Virgin (*Jungfernbastei*), a part of the city fortifications. The old fortifications have been demolished, and only the casemates of the Bastion of the Virgin have been excavated and are open the public. The scenes in Figs. 20 and 21 convey a sense of the environment in which Bottger was forced to carry out his work.

There, the team consisting of Böttger, his five assistants, Tschirnhaus, and the metallurgist Gottfried Pabst von Ohain focused their work on porcelain, and on January 15, 1708, Böttger was able to record the first successes in his lab notebook. According to the chronicles, on March 3, 1709, he was able to present the King with "good white porcelain with the finest glaze," whereupon the King issued him the patent rights for the establishment of a porcelain manufactory inside the Albrechtsburg in Meissen on January 1, 1710. The formula for making porcelain was a closely guarded secret known as the *Arcanum*. Those in possession of the secret were referred to as *arcanists*. Revealing this secret recipe was a crime punishable by death.

Fig. 21. The casemates seen from the inside. Böttger and his assistants labored in dark halls like these.

Fig. 22. The Albrechtsburg today as seen from the ferryboat on the Elbe River.

Fig. 23. "The Presentation of the Arcanum to Prince Elector August" mural in the Albrechtsburg painted by Paul Kießling (1836-1919). The figure behind Böttger represents Tschirnhaus.

The Albrechtsburg in Meissen, the first true palace in the history of German architecture, was commissioned by Duke Albrecht the Brave (Albrecht der Beherzte 1443-1500), who reigned over Saxon lands together with his older brother, Prince Elector Ernst. The Albrechtsburg was designed in 1470 in the manner of a fifteenth century French chateaux by Arnold von Westfalen (1425-1482), who was appointed chief architect (*Baumeister*) to the Dresden Court on June 14, 1471. The palace, which was finally completed in 1524 during the reign of Georg the Bearded (Georg der Bärtige 1500-1539) was given its present-day name in 1676. It still stands today, and is open to visitors. It is three stories high with an irregular ground plan and asymmetric stair towers, and clearly marks the architectural transition from a border fort to a residential Renaissance palace. You can catch glimpses of it in Figs. 22 and 23. Böttger, despite his success in making porcelain, remained technically a prisoner in Dresden until he was granted his freedom in 1714. In 1715 he was awarded the title to the Meissen Porcelain Manufactory. Nevertheless he stayed in Dresden, visiting Meissen only occasionally, and was never formally named as the director of the manufactory. Until his death in 1719, he merely used the title of administrator.

In a much quoted memorandum to King August, dated March 28, 1709, Böttger had promised not just "good white porcelain with the finest of glazes" but "porcelain with all appropriate painting which even if not superior to the East-Indian porcelain, it will at least be equal to it. " (or in the original German of the time, "*das guthe weisse Porcellain samt der allerfeinsten Glasur und allem zubehörigen Mahlwerck, welches dem Ost-Indianischen wo nicht vor, doch wenigstens gleich kommen solle*"). It is noteworthy that Böttger considers Chinese porcelain as the standard of quality against which glaze and painting should be measured. He undoubtedly chose to express himself in a manner pleasing to King August. For in his own mind Böttger, unlike August, actually held Chinese porcelain in low esteem. He characterized Chinese designs as "absurd" and Chinese shapes as "clumsy" (*ungeschickt*). The same is true of Johann Jacob Irminger, the court silversmith who in 1710 was assigned by royal decree to Böttger, and in 1712 was appointed head of the art department, becoming Meissen's first modeler. Irminger worked in the European Rococo tradition emphasizing primarily relief decoration (Figs. 234 and 235). Had Irminger continued to exert influence on Meissen's artistic direction, European shapes and decoration would have undoubtedly been predominant in the early history of porcelain. Following Böttger's death in 1719, Irminger began losing interest in porcelain and left Meissen in 1720, shortly after the arrival of Johann Gregorius Höroldt (1696-1775).

Höroldt, the son of a tailor, was born in Jena. He was a trained artist, having worked as a painter in Strassburg and later in Vienna. In 1719 he started work at the Vienna Porcelain Manufactory, which at the time was still owned privately by the Dutchman Claudius Innocentius du Paquier. The Vienna Factory, known as Royal Vienna after it was acquired by Empress Maria Theresia in 1744, was founded by Du Paquier in 1718 with the help of Konrad Christoph Unger (or Hunger), a Meissen turncoat, claiming to be in possession of the porcelain Arcanum. Unger was joined in 1719 by yet another traitor to Meissen, the arcanist Samuel Stöltzel whom we have already encountered as one of Böttger's early assistants. As a Dutchman, Du Paquier was steeped in the decorating traditions of the Delft faience manufacturers, who were, as discussed previously, heavily influenced by Chinese and Japanese motifs. It is likely that he encouraged Höroldt to concentrate on developing chinoiserie. Stöltzel had defected to Austria, mainly to avoid having to marry the daughter of his landlord who was pregnant with his child. Soon thereafter he wished to return to Meissen.

Revealing the secret of porcelain however was a serious crime punishable by death. To appease King August, Stöltzel proposed to bring in Höroldt, who was already becoming known for developing the technology for brilliant overglaze colors. That suited August well, since under Böttger, the development of porcelain painting had lagged far behind other advances. Nothing in the history of porcelain is uncontroversial, and Unger always maintained that he was the true inventor of porcelain painting, and that Höroldt had stolen it from him and smuggled it to Meissen. Before leaving the Vienna Manufactory, Stöltzel also destroyed the kilns and, chemically speaking, "poisoned" the porcelain ingredients, making them unusable. The result was a damage of 10,000 Thalers to the Du Paquier factory, a considerable setback that undoubtedly further endeared Stöltzel to the Saxon authorities.

Be that as it may, Höroldt's arrival in Meissen in May 1720 was a feather on Stöltzel's cap and, as we shall see later, not the only one. Stöltzel's other great accomplishment was the perfection, first together and then in competition with David Köhler, of underglaze cobalt blue technology. We will have to say more about the discovery of this so-called *blue Arcanum* in Part II.

As we mentioned already, August the Strong was a passionate collector and a connoisseur of art and had amassed a very large porcelain collection. While other European potentates of his time kept their more modest porcelain collections in small rooms, August wanted to fill an entire palace with his. In 1717 August purchased a structure known as the Dutch Palace (*Hollaendisches Palais*) because it was rented out to the Dutch ambassador van Cranenborg during 1715-16. August filled the palace with hundreds of Chinese, Japanese, and later with the best of the fledgling Meissen porcelain. He renamed the structure the Japanese Palace (*Japanisches Palais*) and had plans drawn for its conversion to an even larger building that would house his full collection, comprising in 1731 a staggering 35,798 pieces! King August, however, died on February 1, 1733, and his grander dream was never completely realized. Today the palace is home to the Museum of Prehistory and Anthropology. The Dresden Porcelain Collection has been located in one of the galleries in the Zwinger since 1962.

August's infatuation with Chinese motifs drove the development of chinoiserie decoration on porcelain. Chinoiserie refers to the reproduction of Far Eastern decorative elements including people, landscapes, animals, and flowers in rather imaginative ways that are not exactly replicas of the Chinese or Japanese originals. In September 1720 about 147 of the engravings of Chinese landscapes that had already been used by the Delft painters were supplied to the Meissen painters as an inspiration for their work. By 1745 the Meissen library contained 5,135 copper engravings that served as models. While this number also includes numerous Watteau scenes obtained in 1741, the majority of the engravings represented Oriental landscapes.

PART II
Two Centuries of Meissen Underglaze Blue Decoration

Chapter I

The Early Period: Underglaze Blue Painting and Patterns of the Eighteenth Century

The eighteenth century witnessed the rise of Meissen's underglaze blue porcelain to unmatched heights of artistic and technical excellence in the 1720s and '30s, only to see this glorious enterprise end with the dissolution of the blue painter corps coinciding with the resignation of Manufactory Director Count Camillo Marcolini in late 1813. Changing tastes, war, and social unrest, all contributed to the dramatic rise and fall of blue painting. Technologically, the first third of the eighteenth century saw blue painting develop from its initial, fledgling steps of trial and mostly error into a consistently manufacturable product. Artistically, it was during this time that most of the significant shapes and patterns arose, evolved, and acquired largely the form in which they survive to this day.

This chapter begins with a brief history of blue and white porcelain and its significance to the business of the Royal Manufactory during the eighteenth century. Then we will meet the most significant among the early decorators of underglaze blue porcelain or blue painters (*Blaumaler*) as they were called. The main objective of this chapter is, however, to describe the basic shapes and patterns of eighteenth century underglaze blue painting and examine their origins, symbolism, and early evolution.

History of Blue Underglaze Painting in the Eighteenth Century

Situated in the heart of downtown Dresden, the Zwinger is a magnificent complex of Baroque buildings, fountains, gates, and gardens. It has been compared to Paris' *Jardin des Tuileries* (Gleeson 1988). The buildings on either side of the gate under the glockenspiel made of Meissen porcelain bells (Fig. 24) are home to the Dresden Porcelain Collection. Among the many treasures on display here is the small figurine of a Chinese female dressed in an exquisitely modeled robe and carrying a basket dating to 1715. It is modeled after Chinese originals of a Guanyin (or Kuan Yin), the most popular Bodhisattva (a Buddhist deity) in China. The figurine is decorated in underglaze blue but the quality of the decoration is far less sophisticated than the refined modeling. This item very likely documents the first tentative steps by Köhler towards the development of blue painting under the glaze.

Fig. 24. Dresden, gate leading out of the grounds of the Zwinger. Crowning the gate are the prince electoral crossed swords, the coat-of-arms of the Wettiner that inspired the trademark of the Meissen Porcelain Manufactory, white bells made of Meissen porcelain with a clear resonant ringing make up the glockenspiel, another example of Meissen's public art.

The earliest reported successful attempts at sellable underglaze blue painting in Meissen date back to August 26, 1717, and were first offered to the market in 1718 together with other porcelain goods at the world-famous Leipzig Trade Fair. The city of Leipzig had by then been a center of commerce for at least 700 years. Mentioned already in 1015 AD as the Slavic settlement of Libzi protected by German fortifications, Leipzig was at the crossroads of the *Via Regia* from Paris to Novgorod and *Via Imperii* from Norway to Rome. In 1160 the Wettiner margrave of Meissen, Otto the Rich, conferred city rights upon the fortified settlement. Through a series of imperial decrees Leipzig became the most influential marketplace in the center of Europe, a location where the latest and greatest was traded. This was clearly the place to offer the much-desired blue and white porcelain. Manufacturing success was, however, still very spotty. Based on a list of the unsold inventory, underglaze blue ware composed only a miniscule fraction of the porcelain supply offered for sale. Out of forty-five leaf-shaped dishes and twenty-two ovoid teapots, only one in each category was blue-painted. In 1719 Meissen delivered 3,464 pieces of porcelain to Leipzig for the Spring Trade Fair, among them only three (!) blue ovoid teapots (known as *Straußeneier* or ostrich eggs) like the one shown in Fig. 25.

The story of the Dragoner vases recounted in the previous section makes August the Strong's almost compulsive passion for blue painted porcelain quite palpable. Already in 1717, he had announced a reward of 1,000 Thalers to the first person who could come up with blue porcelain painting like the one on Far Eastern imports. Stöltzel and Köhler had their first success that same year. They both were part of Böttger's original team when the first pieces of European porcelain were pulled out of the kiln on a wintry January day in 1708. Stöltzel and Köhler had continued their collaboration after that memorable day in the *Jungfernbastei*, a collaboration that was later interrupted with Stöltzel's defection to Vienna in January of 1719.

The kingly sum attracted its share of charlatans, as might be expected. The most notorious among them were the Mehlhorns, father and son. The father, Johann George, has been described in a biographical note by Rückert (Rückert 1990, p.51) as a *Schmarotzer*, or what we might call a "leech" in English. He claimed to be in possession of the *Arcanum* or secret of porcelain manufacture and also, together with his son Johann Gottfried, in possession of the secret of cobalt blue painting or the *Blue Arcanum* as it was sometimes called. At least, so they bragged to the local newspaper. The father was retained as an employee of the Manufactory just to keep him quiet. The Meissen personnel records of 1719 indicate that he was receiving a monthly salary of 20 Thalers "though he rendered no services" ("*hat zwar keine Dienste gethan*").

Köhler's contribution to underglaze blue technology was to improve the porcelain paste so that it would retain the blue pigment. The archives indicate that on February 16, 1720, Köhler was able to produce ten tea bowls and saucers on which blue painting had been quite successful. Porcelain by Mehlhorn fired at the same time came out damaged, with most of the blue color having disappeared. In June of 1720 Stöltzel was reinstated in Meissen. He revealed to Köhler his invention of the brown glaze, the capuchin brown (see later discussion of *Kapuzinerbraun*), and a special glaze he had developed that was particularly suitable for underglaze painting. Four months after the arrival of Stöltzel and Höroldt, the yield of blue painted porcelain had improved dramatically. Nevertheless it was difficult for Stöltzel, who earlier had been Köhler's peer, to now be reporting to him. Rivalry and later deep animosity developed between the two. That gave King August a good reason to renege on his promise of the reward of one thousand Thalers. While the Commission (akin to a Board of Directors) in charge of the Manufactory acknowledged their accomplishments, the King promised to reward them only if they openly shared their secrets of the *Blue Arcanum* with each other. At the end neither saw a penny of the reward money. Köhler died on April 30th, 1723. According to Höroldt, Köhler passed the secrets of blue painting on to him in the manner of a "death-bed confession." The circumstances of Köhler's death led to "conspiracy theories," especially since nine of the 82 pages of his laboratory notebook were mysteriously missing. Köhler's wife, suspecting foul play, insisted on an autopsy, and one was conducted, but nothing suspicious was ever found.

The Saxon Court under August the Strong was the primary customer for the blue porcelain. In May 1720 Köhler's first successful pieces were sent to King August in his palace in Warsaw. The King was extremely pleased and let it be known that he wished to see samples of all the new shapes. In particular he expressed a strong desire for monumental pieces. Seven large vases were delivered in August 1720, eight more in December.

The large Oriental vases in August's collection were a constant challenge to the Meissen craftsmen. Any early Meissen porcelain in excess of 20" in height should be regarded as an example of superior craftsmanship. According to Arnold (Arnold 1989), only one thrower, Peter Geithner, Meissen's oldest potter, had the skill to shape objects taller than half a meter (just under 20"). He is credited with the creation of the tallest vase from that period. Truly monumental pieces like the Dragoner Vases could not be manufactured however. It was not known at the time that the cause for this failure was the high kaolin content of the Meissen formulation.

Höroldt himself was very ambivalent about monochrome decorations, particularly underglaze ones. They lacked the vibrancy of polychrome decoration and could not reproduce, at least not during this early period, the fine, almost microscopic details that Höroldt's chinoiserie themes demanded. So right from his first days in Meissen he tried to develop ingenious methods to combine underglaze with overglaze polychrome painting. The resulting pieces are of stunning beauty and particularly difficult to execute. The background scenery is painted in cobalt blue, and the artist, visualizing the final painting, reserves areas prior to painting. Subsequently, overglaze polychrome painting completes the scene.

Figurines or even tableware with figural parts were very rare among the early eighteenth century blue painted creations of the Manufactory. Examples of the latter are given in the last section of this chapter, as we review eighteenth century designs and patterns.

Fig. 25. Ovoid teapot supported by three claw feet known as an ostrich egg, (Meissen, c. 1725), H 6.5", D 3.75", decorated with underglaze blue Indian flowers and birds, crossed swords mark with wavy hilts. This shape with blue and white decoration has been mentioned in the archives since 1719 (*reproduced with permission, Staatliche Kunstsammlungen Dresden Porzellansammlung im Zwinger*).

The first true tea service with uniformly decorated blue pieces was sold to the Court by Höroldt in July 1720 for eleven Thaler. It consisted of an ovoid teapot, two sugar bowls, seven tea bowls and saucers, and a waste bowl. In February 1722 six bowls depicting a Far Eastern seascape were sent to the King. We will encounter these pieces again in our discussion of the work of Meissen's first great blue painter, Johann Caspar Ripp. In May and June 1722 the King received about forty blue and white sets of centerpiece vases. Only five vases of that shipment are in existence today. Between 1725 and 1727 porcelain deliveries to the Saxon Court included about 200 pieces of blue and white porcelain. These included coffee pots, teapots, bottles, knife handles, tureens, chocolate cups and saucers, and bowls of every description. By 1728 the Manufactory had begun warehousing blue decorated tableware of various shapes and sizes for the purpose of assembling complete sets upon request. Nevertheless, during the first half of the eighteenth century, uniformly decorated services were the exception rather than the rule.

Large as these deliveries may seem, they pale in comparison to the order intended for the *Holländisches Palais* (by then renamed *Japanisches Palais*) placed in 1730. The total order of over 700 pieces included one hundred pieces of porcelain with white reserves on blue ground, with blue flowers and landscapes, 200 pieces of blue and white tableware, and 20 blue painted and gilded vases. With the death of August the Strong in 1733, the era of using blue and white porcelain for decorative purposes came to an end. Still, the production of blue painted porcelain continued strong. By 1737 the production ratio was 259,620 pieces of white ware intended for overglaze decoration to 178,351 underglaze decorated pieces.

After that date, the significance of underglaze blue porcelain shifted from standalone decorative objects to tableware. For example, when Maria Amalia, daughter of King August III, married Charles IV of the House of Bourbon, King of Naples and Sicily (and later as Charles III King of Spain) on May 9, 1738 (we already discussed the sumptuous festivities), the bridegroom's mother, Elisabeth Farnese, received two large blue and white sets for tea and coffee. Listed among the holdings of the Royal Confectionary in 1773 is a large blue and white set consisting of more than 900 pieces.

The annual sales of the Royal Manufactory rose from 9,694 Thalers in 1720 to 222,560 Thalers in 1752. Unfortunately the Seven Years War (1756-63) between Prussia and Saxony had a disastrous long-term effect on the Manufactory. The immediate financial impact was not all that grave. Initially, the Manufactory income recovered rather quickly. By 1765 it again employed 731 people, among them 77 blue painters. By 1766 the annual income reached 221,500 Thalers, approaching prewar levels. But the war did significant insidious damage that became evident in the decades that followed. During the Seven Years War production at the Meissen Manufactory had come to a standstill. Some of the furnaces were destroyed during the war. The Manufactory's detailed archives from the period disappeared. That gave KPM in Berlin and the now Royal Manufactory in Vienna (under direct ownership of Empress Maria Theresia since 1744) breathing room to assert themselves in the market place. More significantly, many of the artists and arcanists were sent to Frankfurt where they were safe from being forcefully transferred to Berlin. The dislocation caused an interruption in the development of new technology for lowering costs and keeping the Manufactory competitive, and of new designs more suitable to the changing tastes of the late eighteenth century.

After the war King Friedrich II of Prussia, until then a major Meissen customer, banned the sale of Meissen porcelain anywhere in the territories controlled by the Prussian state. The Prussian ban was followed by similar bans on the part of Austria, Denmark, Sweden, and Portugal in a protectionist attempt to bolster their own state and royal manufactories. France, Russia, England, and Spain imposed import taxes of up to sixty percent. The fortunes of the Manufactory entered a period of prolonged decline. Already by 1770 the annual income had shrunk to a mere 24,378 Thalers. It was not until 1866, i.e. late into the nineteenth century, that the Manufactory was once again able to register an annual income in excess of two hundred thousand Thalers. Blue painting fared particularly poorly under these developments. Royal Vienna and KPM could meet the demand for blue porcelain in German-speaking lands. The Saxon nobility was no longer interested in it. The Red Ming Dragon and Yellow Lion patterns increased in popularity, eclipsing the desire for blue painted ware. Wedgwood emerged as an unexpected competitor for blue ware and severely undercut Meissen in price. The invention of inexpensive transfer-printing in Great Britain in 1750 was another factor that impacted Meissen adversely. By 1759 English potters were applying underglaze blue transfer prints to porcelain, and by 1784 Spode had perfected underglaze blue transfer printing on earthenware. These considerably less expensive wares had a major disruptive influence on the mid-range market.

There was also a second, deeper reason, besides pure economics, that brought an end to the first period of underglaze blue painting at Meissen. Already in the last decade of the eighteenth century the Rococo style was losing ground to the emerging Neo-Classicism in the decorative arts. The reader need think only of the shift from the Chippendale style (sometimes called American Rococo) to the Federal and Empire styles in early American furniture. The manner of underglaze blue painting as practiced by Meissen was not suitable for neoclassical shapes and designs.

To reverse its declining fortunes, Prince-Elector Friedrich August III (known as August the Just and a great grandson of August the Strong) brought the Manufactory in 1774 under the administration of Count Camillo Marcolini. Most of the blue tableware during the first part of the Marcoloni period was exported to Russia with single orders of up to 40,000 Thalers. In 1806, when Saxony decided to leave the German Reich, side with Napoleon, and join the *Rheinbund*, Russia completely barred the importation of Meissen porcelain. This last development, together with the change in tastes in Western Europe, marked the end of the first glorious period of blue painting in Meissen. It re-emerged triumphantly, however, in the middle of the nineteenth century as part of the overall Rococo Revival movement in the decorative arts.

The Blue Painters, Organization of The *Blaue Stube* (Blue Room), and the Rising Role of Women

Porcelain painters were generally paid meager wages and led a rather austere life. Their limited diet for example consisted of rye bread, porridge, cabbage soup, buttermilk, and occasionally beer (though some were also reprimanded as being drunkards). But they were still better off than men employed in other trades and infantry or cavalrymen.

Meissen workers were divided in three categories. The more important ones and especially those who were in possession of the *Arcanum* were salaried employees. Formers, molders, and painters were paid by the piece. Unskilled workers whose jobs were not directly related to porcelain manufacturing were hourly employees.

From 1720 to 1730 the porcelain painters were not officially Meissen employees. They worked directly for Höroldt, who ran the painting shop as a subsidiary of the Royal Meissen Manufactory. This subcontracting arrangement lasted until 1730. After 1731, Höroldt was appointed as a regular employee with an annual salary of 1,000 Thalers. Formers and painters made in comparison 80-260 Thalers. Nevertheless the company was rather progressive in its structure. Salaried employees received a sick pay of one Thaler per week and there was a pension plan and survivor's benefits for the widows until they remarried. Apprentices received a small salary as a stipend while in training. Once they began producing sellable ware, they were paid by the piece.

A detailed biographical section covering all blue painters of the eighteenth century would far exceed the scope of this book. Featuring some of the more important ones, however, together with examples of their work can help convey to the reader a deeper understanding of the various artistic influences on them.

Höroldt's intent had always been to hire apprentices already initiated to the art of blue painting on Delftware. He was personally not particularly fond of blue painting (he has been quoted as saying that blue painting "...was not his thing" cf. Arnold 1989). He hired many of the early blue painters out of the Dresdener Faience Manufactory of Peter Eggebrecht. Eggebrecht was probably trained in Delft, had worked for a pottery in Berlin, and in 1710 he joined the pottery founded by Böttger in Dresden. Soon thereafter he leased the factory, and later acquired outright ownership of it, eventually creating the Dresdener Faience Manufactory.

Johann Caspar Ripp was the pioneer among Meissen's blue painters. Born in 1681 in Hanau, he was trained in Holland as a faience painter in the Delft (i.e. blue-and-white) style. He worked in potteries in Frankfurt, Hanau, Ansbach, Nürnberg, and other places before joining Eggebrecht's Faience Manufactory. Ripp and Höroldt negotiated through Stöltzel, and in 1720 Ripp was hired with the promise of getting all the blue painting assignments together with helpers and apprentices. Ripp proved extremely productive, delivering together with his crew over 4,800 pieces in less than twelve months. But he was also fiercely independent. He proposed to the Meissen Manufactory that he work directly for them rather than as a subcontractor through Höroldt. All this roused Höroldt's envy and anger, and led to Ripp's dismissal on a technicality in 1723. His brief tenure in Meissen renders his work rare and highly desirable.

Johann Christoph Horn (1692-1760) was the brother-in-law of Eggebrecht and apprenticed at the Dresdener Faience Manufactory. He was hired into Meissen by Höroldt in 1720 against Eggebrecht's wishes. In 1730, his annual salary including overtime was about 220 Thalers. Later he made up to 272 Thalers annually when paid by piecework. A document from 1731 cites Horn's job description as "painter in blue and polychrome Japanese figures and flowers." He is credited with painting the pear-shaped jug shown in Fig. 26 and possibly the plate in Fig. 27. Besides Ripp and Horn, Höroldt hired two other blue painters away from Eggebrecht, Johann Christian Hamann and Johann Ehrenfried Stadler.

Fig. 26. Pear-shaped jug (Meissen, c. 1722-23) combined under and overglaze decoration attributed to Johann Christoph Horn. H 6.5", lid is Chinese export porcelain and not original to the piece. The water and the landscape and town skyline in the background are in underglaze blue. Polychrome overglaze decoration in yellow, green, gray, and rust red depicting a bathing scene with scantily clad ladies helped into the water by a naked man. The blue and polychrome painting had to be done in tandem, proof that this is not the work of outside decorators or *Hausmaler* (*reproduced with permission, Staatliche Kunstsammlungen Dresden Porzellansammlung im Zwinger*).

In view of the steadily growing demand for blue and white porcelain, inspector Steinbrück recommended in 1723 that Höroldt assign more painters to this task. By 1725 the blue painter corps consisted of nine journeymen (*Gesellen*) and five apprentices. By 1729 the number had risen to twenty-four. When the painters became regular employees of the manufactory after 1730, all the blue painters were paid by piecework. Only the oldest one, Friedrich August Zimmermann was made into a salaried employee.

After 1731 the number of blue painters increased dramatically. By 1735 there were forty-seven blue painters, including apprentices. By 1739 the total number of painters had already increased to seventy. It was decided to subdivide the painters into four to six separate groups, each under the supervision of a senior painter. By 1744 there were fifty-three blue painters and the number of blue painter apprentices alone had risen to twenty. In 1745 Höroldt put the latter together in the so-called first Blue Room (*Blaue Stube*) under the supervision of Peter Kolmberger. The senior blue painters were grouped together in a second Blue Room under the supervision of Carl Friedrich Eggebrecht, son of Peter Eggebrecht, who was mentioned earlier. Familiarity with the foremen of the Blue Room is of more than just academic significance. As we shall see presently, it contributes to the correct interpretation of some markings on blue and white porcelain of this period.

The list of the foremen (their years of service in parenthesis) is:

Peter Kolmberger (1745-1779) supervising the Blue Room for apprentices.

Carl Friedrich Eggebrecht (1745-1749) supervising the Blue Room for senior painters. His position was not filled after he returned to painting in 1749.

Johann Carl Möbius, Sr. (July 7-August 15, 1780) was a very highly regarded painter but he only served for five weeks as foreman. He was convicted of embezzlement and terminated.

Johann Gottlieb Hahnefeld, Sr. (1780-1785).

Johann Christian Zschentzsch (1785-1802).

Fig. 27. Flat plate (Meissen c. 1722-23) underglaze blue floral and stylized rock decoration with chinoiserie painted over the glaze, attributed to Johann Christoph Horn (*reproduced with permission, Staatliche Kunstsammlungen Dresden Porzellansammlung im Zwinger*).

Johann Benjamin Foerster (July 7, 1802-November 28, 1802 deceased).

Johan Gottlieb Möbius (1802-1828), last foreman of the Blue Room when it closed in 1814. Retained as foreman of the green underglaze painters after 1817 (see section on the nineteenth century for details).

A systematic discussion of the Meissen marks is given in Part III of this book. There is so much variability in the early marks, however, that their details are best presented as part of the descriptions of individual eighteenth century pieces. Many pieces from this time frame have letters and, sometimes, Roman numerals in underglaze blue just under the crossed swords marks. The significance of these letters has been the subject of heated debate among scholars. There are essentially three main competing conjectures as to the meaning of these markings and they all probably contain a grain of truth (see for example Röntgen 1996, Röntgen 2004, Röntgen's contribution in Arnold 1989) and are summarized below:

Conjecture #1: The letters are internal manufactory symbols for various experimental formulations. This is known to be true for the letters B, E, and W but only during 1788-89. The arcanists Busch, Elsässer, and Walther had developed new glazes and it was important to identify the pieces to see how they reacted to the second (sharp) firing.

Conjecture #2: The letters are the initials of the Blue Room foremen, signing off on a piece, a sort of quality control. There are many more letters than the above list of foremen can account for. Furthermore, the initials Mö for example occur frequently enough that they cannot possibly signify work done under Möbius' short tenure as foreman, they more likely reflect work actually painted by him. This brings us to ...

Conjecture #3: The letters are actually initials of the blue painters themselves. This is the most commonly accepted interpretation and one that we will adhere to when describing marks on individual selected pieces. The fact that several painters had the same initial is a source of confusion and has given rise to many scholarly discussions as to the correct attribution. The letter "K" in particular appears to be the target of much debate.

So do letters signify painters' initials? The answer seems to be, most often they do, but sometimes they don't! Letters alone cannot always be used to identify the painter and thus roughly date a piece. Instead, the dating should be done first based on other criteria. Only then, and only if the date of the piece and the dates that a blue painter with that particular initial served in the Manufactory overlap, can one attempt a plausible attribution to that painter.

The fact that blue painters were allowed to sign their pieces is rather unusual. In general the Meissen Manufactory strongly discouraged its artists from signing their work. Disciplinary action might have been taken against those who did. Some tried to circumvent this restriction in extremely innovative and artful ways. A case in point is described in the recent literature (Stümpfle-Wolf 2005). In 1725-30 the painter Philip Ernst Schindler was able to work his initials PES masterfully into the splat of a chair painted as part of a chinoiserie scene. The scene is painted on a plate about 6 3/4" in diameter. The entire three-letter initial is less than 1/8" across, yet perfectly crisp when viewed with a magnifying glass. The plate is part of the Schneider collection and on exhibit in Schloss Lustheim in Oberschleissheim, a suburb of Munich. So why were the blue painters allowed to openly sign their work? The thousands of pages of the Meissen Archives are simply silent on this matter. A likely answer is that the initials were not applied for the purpose of satisfying the vanity of the painter. That was simply an unintended consequence. The real reason was more likely to keep count of a given painter's output, since blue painters were paid by the piece.

Before we conclude our discussion of the eighteenth century blue painters, we must touch upon the rising importance of women artists in the Manufactory during this period. The Manufactory did not employ any women in the production or painting of porcelain until after the Seven Years' War. As Saxony began to rebuild there was increased demand for porcelain, particularly for blue and white dinnerware to replace whatever was lost during the turmoil of the war. It was suggested that the daughters and wives of production personnel (*Manufakturisten*) could be hired to do some of the simpler painting tasks, polish gold, and shape handles, all of them tasks that did not require lengthy training.

Seventeen women were hired for the first time by the Manufactory in 1765. Fifteen of those were admitted to blue painting. Women were paid one third of a male employee's salary Nevertheless their numbers rose steadily. By 1769 there were thirty-seven women employees, in 1774 their number had increased to fifty-three, with ten employed as blue painters. Women painters had their own room and eventually female supervisors. The first female painter joined the Manufactory on January 15, 1765. She was Caroline Sophia Heinrici, daughter of the painter Johann Martin Heinrici. She worked initially as blue painter and later as gilder until her marriage on May 21, 1784.

Eighteenth Century Designs and Patterns

The designs and patterns of eighteenth century blue and white porcelain, primarily those of the Meissen Manufactory, are characterized by an enormous diversity reflecting both Far Eastern and European influences. Scholars have used different schemes to classify and catalog the various patterns. Some of these schemes are quite intricate and involved. A simpler approach to classification will be used here. First we shall make a distinction between Far Eastern and European designs. The Far Eastern patterns can be further divided into scenes of everyday life and architecture, floral motifs and avian motifs. There is a symbolic significance to many of the Far Eastern motifs, though it is far from certain that the Meissen painters were actually aware of the symbolism. It is more likely that they were faithfully copying antecedents on imported Oriental porcelain or seventeenth century European faience.

European patterns, the second category of our survey, include German flowers, highly stylized floral motifs, and the inimitable "frolicking putti." In the following we shall give examples of each pattern and discuss it in terms of origin, symbolism, and variants including many detailed pictures. Whenever possible, pictures of Far Eastern or European antecedents that served as sources of inspiration will also be given. In his recent book Hans Sonntag (Sonntag 1999) has discussed extensively the symbolic meanings of Far Eastern motifs on Meissen porcelain.

A third category comprises pieces that have been overdecorated either by gilding or additional overglaze painting of the finished product. Even though a whole section of the book is dedicated to a general discussion of porcelain marks, we have chosen to depict many representative eighteenth century marks together with the piece on which they are found. The German names for the various patterns are given in parentheses, primarily to facilitate the search of the German auction market by English speaking collectors.

Motifs with Far Eastern Places and Figures (*Chinoiserie*):

The fascination with Far Eastern motifs in the decoration of European pottery and polychrome Meissen decorations was echoed also in the decoration of blue and white porcelain. The recurring themes are people living in harmony while attending everyday chores, surrounded by serene landscapes and structures in alien architectural styles. The sources for these motifs were accounts and drawings by travelers to the Far East, existing designs on European blue and white faience, and of course Chinese export porcelain originals.

Far Eastern Fisherman (*Chinesischer Angler*):

The depiction of fishermen on a background of Chinese flowers, rocks, trees, and waterfowl is a recurring theme borrowed directly from Chinese export porcelain as evidenced by the Kangxi period bowl of Fig. 30. The border on the ledge surrounding the central painting in the well of the bowl can be seen in very early Meissen pieces. A similar motif, possibly Japanese-inspired and commonly encountered on mid-eighteenth century tea bowls, is a pair of fishermen exchanging a basket, presumably containing the day's catch. Several views of such a piece are shown in Figs. 31-35. Also interesting is the hatched motif of the border. This motif can be seen on Chinese porcelain of the Kangxi period. It is very likely the basis for one of the decorative elements of the Strawflower pattern we will discuss later. The mark on this item also includes the blue painter initial "K" which has been attributed to Kretzschmar or, as von Barsewisch more plausibly suggests (von Barsewisch 1988), to Kohnberger. Be that as it may, the initial "K" is significant for it has been associated with the earliest examples of the Blue Onion pattern.

Teahouse in Oriental Garden (*Chinesischer Garten mit Teehaus*):

Von Barsewisch calls this motif "Pagoda and Three Trees" (*Pagode und drei Bäume*). The exterior of the cups, saucers, and other utensils in this design is often coated in a dark brown glaze known as Capuchin brown, named after the color of the hood worn by Franciscan monks of the Capuchin order. The glaze, developed by Stöltzel in 1720, is based on iron oxide. Its purpose, according to Sterba (Sterba 1989), was to give utilitarian porcelain pieces the familiar feel of everyday pottery and stoneware, though the attraction of such a disguise is not entirely clear. The very early plate (or saucer) of Fig. 28 by Ripp discussed previously, a piece intended for King August himself, was similarly glazed (cf. Fig. 29).

Fig. 28. Saucer (Meissen, 1721) decorated with a rocky coastline, sailboats, and water fowl in an Asian setting in underglaze blue. D 7.75". This is one of six such saucers presented to King August in February of 1722. The design is taken from earlier Dutch faience and is also known from faience tiles decorated in Dresden (*reproduced with permission, The Gardiner Museum of Ceramic Art, Toronto Canada*).

Fig. 29. Underside of the saucer in Fig. 28 showing the capuchin brown glaze, see Fig. 342 for a discussion of the marks (*reproduced with permission, The Gardiner Museum of Ceramic Art, Toronto Canada*).

Fig. 30. Bowl (Chinese, Kangxi Period, c. 1700) underglaze blue decoration with fishermen, D 6.5", these simple scenic motifs were copied by faience and early porcelain painters (estimated value $150-175).

Fig. 31. Tea bowl and saucer (Meissen c. 1730-40) decorated in underglaze blue with Chinese fishermen, bowl H 1.38", saucer D 3.38" (estimated value $2,000-2,750).

Fig. 32. Side view of tea bowl in Fig. 31. The stylized prunus tree is also found in the Rock and Bird Pattern.

Fig. 34. Tea bowl of Fig. 31, view of the inside. The Indian flower is typically also found in the bottoms of cups decorated in other Far Eastern patterns such as the Strawflower and Rock and Bird. The striate decoration around the inside of the rim has been borrowed by the Strawflower Pattern.

Fig. 33. Side view of the tea bowl in Fig. 31. The fishermen are drawn as Oriental in a much more convincing manner than in polychrome chinoiserie.

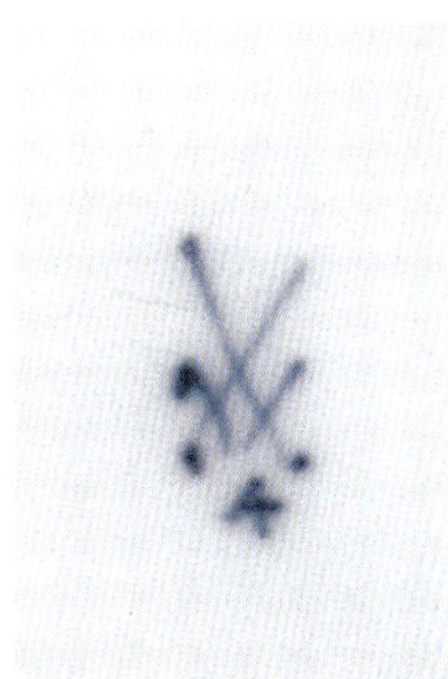

Fig. 35. Mark on tea bowl of Fig. 31 showing painter's initial "K" ascribed to either Kolmberger or Kretzschmar.

This Chinese scenery shows a pagoda or possibly a gazebo-like structure placed in a serene garden environment flanked by three trees, one of them an evergreen (Figs. 36 - 38). The motif is consistent with the utopian view of a distant land living in peace and harmony. The evergreen tree in the middle has also a symbolic meaning, standing for longevity and resilience. A similar pattern in overglaze polychrome painting is found on a dinner service made around 1735 for Count Johann Christian von Hennicke (Sterba 1989).

Chinese Figures on Meissen Tiles:

The manufactory archives indicate that Meissen produced large quantities of tiles during the first half of the eighteenth century. They are practically non-existent today. The only two known surviving specimens are in the von Barsewisch collection and are shown in Figs. 39 and 40. Both tiles were made after 1740 (impressed former numbers). The tile in Fig. 39 depicts the Chinese Goddess of the Heavens riding a buck and has also been encountered on faience painting by Adam Friedrich von Löwenfinck, the eldest of the three Löwenfinck brothers, two of them Meissen deserters. The tile in Fig. 40 derives from the cover of a series of chinoiserie engravings by the Dutchman Petrus Schenk.

Fig. 37. Detail of the saucer in Fig. 36 showing the stylized Oriental landscape as the central motif, also repeated inside the cup.

Fig. 36. Cup and saucer (Meissen, c. 1750), both pieces underglaze blue decorated in the Pagoda and Three Trees pattern on a fluted or ribbed relief body (*gebrochener Stab*), saucer D 5", cup D 2.75", H 1.75" (estimated value $950-1,100).

Fig. 38. Bottom view of the cup of Fig. 36, showing the capuchin brown glaze (attributed to Stöltzel), crossed swords mark with dot and wavy hilts.

Fig. 39. Tile (Meissen, c. 1740): Underglaze blue chinoiserie depicting the Chinese goddess of the heavens. L 5.25" (Courtesy of the Dr. B. von Barsewisch Collection/Schlossmuseum Wolfshagen Prignitz).

Fig. 40. Tile (Meissen, c. 1740): Underglaze blue chinoiserie after Petrus Schenck. L 5.25". Companion piece to Fig. 39 (Courtesy of the Dr. B. von Barsewisch Collection/Schlossmuseum Wolfshagen Prignitz).

Chinese Figures in Imaginary Architectural Settings (*Chinesen und Phantasiearchitektur*):

This particular pattern shows Chinese figures in architectural settings that are more the product of Western artistic license than anything a traveler might have encountered in China or Japan at that time. All known pieces were decorated around 1770. The pattern has surfaced relatively recently, and is thus of special significance to collectors. Until the early 1970s it was known primarily on round and oval covered butter dishes. Extensive Meissen blue and white dinner services from the eighteenth century are extremely rare, few were produced, and fewer yet seem to have survived. It was thus a great surprise when numerous pieces in this pattern, both place settings and serving pieces, were unexpectedly offered at auction around 1973. All pieces are initialed by the blue painters "K" (probably Kolmberger) or "Mö" (most likely Möbius, Sr.). Today these items are being held in two private collections, in a collection in Aachen (cf. Reiff 1986) and in the von Barsewisch Collection in Schlossmuseum Wolfshagen, Prignitz. The latter is covered extensively in this book. The pieces from this set currently in the von Barsewisch collection include two covered tureens with underplates (underplate shown in Fig. 41), two covered round bowls with underplates, two large round platters, two large plates, a meat platter (shown in Fig. 42), and numerous dinner plates, soup bowls, and dessert plates.

The dinner service does not consist uniformly of a single shape. The tureens with their twisted finials and the underplate of Fig. 41 are in the "New Cutout" (*Neuer Ausschnitt*) shape,

Fig. 41. Tureen underplate (Meissen, c. 1774) decorated with Chinese figures in an imaginary architectural setting, crossed swords over "K", L 13.75" (*Courtesy of the Dr. B. von Barsewisch Collection/Schlossmuseum Wolfshagen Prignitz*).

designed in 1745 by the legendary modeler Johann Joachim Kaendler. This shape gained its popularity in the nineteenth century with the resurgence of the Blue Onion pattern and will be discussed in the next chapter. The plates and bowls with their smooth rims, on the other hand, are typical of the plainer shape more common during the earlier part of the eighteenth century.

This pattern has a significant distinguishing feature. It is one of the very few underglaze blue patterns that can be traced back to the original Höroldt drawings. A collection of 124 such drawings can be examined today by permission and under the watchful eye of the curators in the library of the Grassi Museum in Leipzig. Nearly half the drawings are believed to be in Höroldt's own hand. They were given out to the painters to copy or use as stencils. The drawings languished in a drawer in the Meissen Manufactory until they somehow fell into the hands of two famous collectors, Georg Wilhelm Schulz and Adolf List. The Grassi Museum acquired them from the Schulz family. Known today collectively as the Schulz-Codex, they represent a priceless document of the history of porcelain.

Fig. 42. Meat platter (Meissen, c. 1774) decorated with Chinese figures in an imaginary architectural setting, crossed swords over "K", L 17.5", W 13" (*Courtesy of the Dr. B. von Barsewisch Collection/Schlossmuseum Wolfshagen Prignitz*).

Chinese Flower Motifs (including *Indianische Blumen*):

Chinese painting is two-dimensional with no attempt to represent depth, the rendering of volume being predominantly if not exclusively an attribute of Western painting. While other typical painting styles, such as *deutsche Blumen* or *ombrierte Blumen*, convey volume, decors like the Indian Flowers (*indianische Blumen*) pattern and of course the Blue Onion (*Zwiebelmuster*) pattern are two dimensional, belying their Asian origins. Figs. 43-45 illustrate the close connection between Chinese and Meissen floral motifs on blue and white porcelain.

Fig. 43. Plate with Oriental flower basket. Chinese. Kangxi period, late 17th century. D 9". This underglaze blue basket can be regarded as an Oriental antecedent of the Meissen version shown in Fig. 44.

Fig. 44. Plate (Meissen, c. 1730-40) Chinese flower basket. D 9" (*Courtesy of the Dr. B. von Barsewisch Collection/Schlossmuseum Wolfshagen Prignitz*).

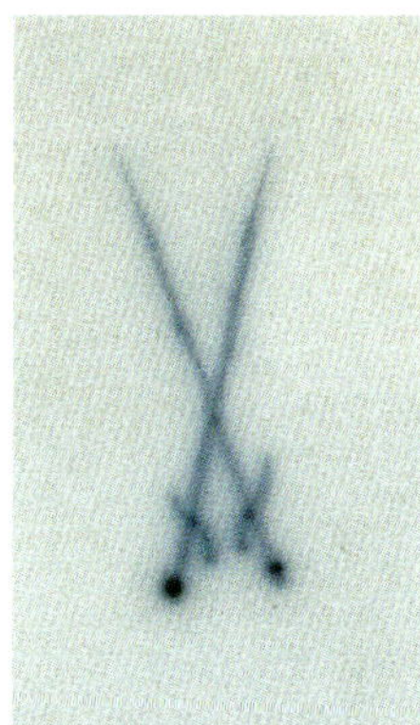

Fig. 45. Crossed swords mark on plate of Fig. 44, also incised X at foot rim. (*Courtesy of the Dr. B. von Barsewisch Collection/Schlossmuseum Wolfshagen Prignitz*).

Peonies and chrysanthemums are the two most significant Far Eastern flower motifs. On Meissen pieces they appear either individually or as parts of a more complex composition, such as the Blue Onion pattern. These two flowers are often drawn in a highly stylized manner, so much so that a quick differentiation between the two is not always easy. The square washbasin from the von Barsewisch Collection shown in Fig. 46 is particularly instructive because it shows both flowers side by side. The flower design on the left is generally interpreted as a chrysanthemum and is characterized by lozenge-shaped petals. The serrated petals of the floral design on the right make it a peony. The same representation of a peony appears also on the Rock and Bird pattern.

The wash basin has two additional motifs that are widely encountered on Meissen chinoiserie. One is the fence structure, the other the perforated object that is representative of the Chinese convoluted limestones traditionally used in China as three-dimensional decorative objects. The rendering of the rock on this item is closer to the Chinese rocks (cf. Fig. 97) than the rocks on the Rock and Bird pattern discussed later. A stein dating to 1740-1750, and similarly decorated with chrysanthemum, a peony, a rock, and a fence, was recently sold by the Auction House Bergmann. The stein is shown in Fig. 47.

Fig. 46. Washbasin (Meissen, c. 1740-50). Underglaze blue chrysanthemum (left), peony (right) with rock and fence. L 11", W 9.5". Crossed swords mark with blue painter's initial "K", also impressed number 27. (*Courtesy of the Dr. B. von Barsewisch Collection/Schlossmuseum Wolfshagen Prignitz*).

Fig. 47. Tankard with lid (Meissen c. 1740-50), decorated in underglaze blue with a chrysanthemum, rock, and peony over a fence, the lid often added later, H 10.25", bottom unglazed, minor repairs to the rim, crossed swords mark is shown in the inset (*courtesy of Auktionshaus Bergmann, Erlangen, Germany*) (estimated value as $6,500-7,500).

Another instructive example from the von Barsewisch Collection is the helmet-shaped pitcher shown in Figs. 48-50. The side view shows a stylized peony, also viewed sideways. The front view shows the stem of a bamboo tree and wound around it a flower stem terminating in a chrysanthemum.

Fig. 49. Frontal view of pitcher in Fig. 48. Bamboo and chrysanthemum. (Courtesy of the Dr. B. von Barsewisch Collection/ Schlossmuseum Wolfshagen Prignitz).

Fig. 48. Helmet-shaped pitcher (Meissen, c. 1740-50). Underglaze blue peonies in side view. H 8". (Courtesy of the Dr. B. von Barsewisch Collection/Schlossmuseum Wolfshagen Prignitz).

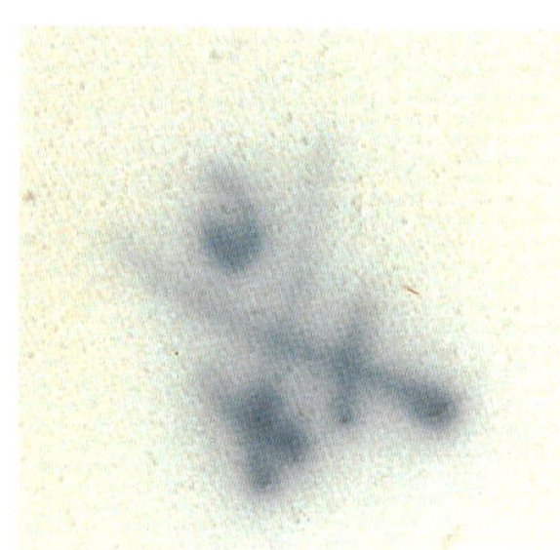

Fig. 50. Mark on pitcher of Fig. 48. Asymmetric crossed swords with blue painter's initial "O" above the blades. (Courtesy of the Dr. B. von Barsewisch Collection/Schlossmuseum Wolfshagen Prignitz).

Fig. 51. Covered tureen with fish handles (Meissen, c. 1730-40) decorated with Indian Flowers and birds in flight, crossed swords over "K", H (without lid) 4", D (inner) 8.75" (Courtesy of the Dr. B. von Barsewisch Collection/Schlossmuseum Wolfshagen Prignitz).

Fig. 52. Detail of the fish handle in Fig. 51 (Courtesy of the Dr. B. von Barsewisch Collection/Schlossmuseum Wolfshagen Prignitz).

The Indian Flower Pattern (*Indianische Blumen*):

Highly stylized flowers painted in a manner emulating Far Eastern originals are common motifs on pottery and porcelain from most manufactories. During the second quarter of the eighteenth century this motif was painted in an elaborate and artistically painstaking manner. Two particularly graceful examples from the von Barsewisch collection are shown here. A Meissen covered tureen, ca. 1730-40, with carefully modeled fish handles is shown in Figs. 51 and 52.

A Meissen covered pot with figural handles and an acorn finial, ca. 1730-40, is shown in Fig. 53. The classic European faces on the handles are in juxtaposition to the Chinese-inspired decoration. This mixing of Western and Oriental decorative elements has persisted throughout the nineteenth century up to the present.

After 1740, the Indian Flower pattern in underglaze blue becomes increasingly simplified, finally giving rise to the widely popular and utilitarian Strawflower pattern discussed later in this chapter. Another example of the kinship between the Indian Flower and the Strawflower patterns is afforded by the rare and unusual spittoon from the Gardiner Museum ca. 1760-75 shown in Fig. 54. Similarly, the decoration on an eggcup from the Marcolini period (ca. 1774-1814) in the Indian Flower Pattern can be seen as transitional to the Strawflower pattern (cf. Figs. 55 and 56).

Fig. 53. Lidded pot with handles (Meissen, c. 1730-40) decorated with Indian Flowers, the handles with masks of European women, acorn finial on the lid, crossed swords with "S" between wavy hilts, H 12.75" (*Courtesy of the Dr. B. von Barsewisch Collection/Schlossmuseum Wolfshagen Prignitz*).

Fig. 55. Eggcup (Meissen c. 1775-1814) decorated in underglaze blue Indian Flowers, H 2.75" (estimated value $250-325).

Fig. 56. Mark on the eggcup of Fig. 55, crossed swords with star, in use during the Marcolini period beginning with 1775, the second year of his directorship.

Fig. 54. Spittoon (Meissen c. 1760-75) having a globular body with wide rim and handle with molded palmetto leaves and animal head end that serves as spout for emptying the contents, decorated in underglaze blue with Indian Flowers and Insects, marked with crossed swords with dot and painter's initial "T", L 8" *(reproduced with permission The Gardiner Museum of Ceramic Art, Toronto Canada)*.

Fig. 57. Plate (China, Kangxi Period, c. 1700), Chinese antecedent of the Blue Pattern with striking similarities to the "three-fruit" variant, with realistically drawn pomegranate, peach, and citrus fruit, central flower, a chrysanthemum with pollen as well as the ledge decoration match early Blue Onion, D 8.75" *(reproduced with permission Hetjens Museum, Düsseldorf Germany)*.

The Blue Onion Pattern (*Zwiebelmuster*):

Recognized instantly by novice and experienced collectors alike, the Blue Onion pattern is undoubtedly the most popular pattern in the history of porcelain. This pattern brings together many Far Eastern aesthetic elements rich in symbolism. As was mentioned earlier, the ruling elites were well versed in art and literature and appreciative of subtle symbolism on festive occasions. The motifs of the pattern may have triggered many learned or even suggestive and flirtatious conversations during the sumptuous feasts. We do not know whether the eighteenth century Meissen blue painters themselves fully appreciated the symbolic meaning of the motifs they copied from Chinese originals. Early eighteenth century pieces do however differ significantly from each other, as well as from their Oriental antecedents, reflecting the individuality of the artists and the rapid evolution of the Blue Onion pattern during these years. By the time the Blue Onion pattern reached the climax of its phenomenal success in the second half of the nineteenth century it had already become highly standardized. While still rich in symbolism and detail, these nineteenth century pieces are fairly uniform and were intended to be readily assembled into dinner sets of various sizes. Even so, as we saw earlier, one still notices variations among them. It is these irregularities in the application of the pattern that have contributed to its charm, which has persisted undiminished for over two centuries.

The Blue Onion pattern is not only the most popular of the blue and white patterns, it is also the most complex. Nevertheless, it can be painted in such a way as to cover the most diverse shapes and irregular surfaces in an esthetically pleasing manner despite its complexity. Typically it is plates and platters that display all of the decorative elements and all of the known Chinese antecedents are flat objects. For that reason we will use plates from various periods to discuss the decorative motifs. In terms of its decoration, a Blue Onion plate can be separated into three distinct areas, the edge, the ledge, and the well. The motifs on each of these areas will be discussed individually.

Before we discuss the individual design elements, however, some general remarks on the Chinese originals are in order. Only a few such examples are known (although some of the motifs can be seen on related decorations). A total of three polychrome and five blue and white examples of Chinese porcelain with the Blue Onion pattern have been reported so far (Miedtank 2001). One of them, currently in the Hetjens Museum in Düsseldorf, is shown in Fig. 57.

A Chinese overdecorated plate with underglaze blue and overglaze red painting sharing some of the Blue Onion elements can be seen at the Peabody Essex Museum in Salem, Massachusetts. This piece is significant because it bears a Johanneum number, i.e. an inventory number of the royal porcelain collection in Dresden, implying it was owned by August the Strong. The archives mention that Chinese porcelain items from the palace in Dresden were regularly sent to Meissen to be used as models by the painters. The plate and its inventory number are shown in Figs. 58 and 59.

Fig. 58. Plate (Chinese, c. 1700) decorated with a central chrysanthemum, peonies, and a pomegranate in underglaze blue and overglaze rust red and yellow with gold highlights (*reproduced with permission, Peabody Essex Museum, Salem MA*).

Fig. 59. Underside of the plate in Fig. 58 showing the Johanneum number 146, evidence of royal provenance. Johanneum numbers are inventory numbers on pieces from the collection of King August the Strong (*reproduced with permission, Peabody Essex Museum, Salem MA*).

Edge motifs: The edge decoration of both Chinese and Meissen or other European renditions of the Blue Onion pattern consists of fruits separated by flowers and foliage. Note that *none of these fruits is intended to be an onion!* The word *Zwiebelmuster* meaning onion pattern is a colloquialism introduced late in the eighteenth century and translated into English as Blue Onion. To repeat, there is no onion in Blue Onion. On the Chinese original from the Hetjens Museum three different fruits separate the border into three sections, decorated symmetrically with leaves and flowers in between the fruits. These have been interpreted as the three "blessed fruits," the pomegranate, the peach, and the mandarin orange (or a related citrus fruit). Their meaning is deeply rooted in the symbolism of Chinese aesthetics and mythology. The stems of the three fruits point outwards, towards the circular rim of the plate and thus define a circle circumscribing a triangle. The circle with no beginning or end symbolizes the eternal cycles of life and nature, the triangle stands for birth, life, and death or past, present, and future.

The oldest known Meissen Blue Onion piece, a plate dating to 1728-1730, is very similar to this Chinese original. Originally preserved in shards in the Rudolf Just collection, it has now been restored and resides with a private Berlin collection. A picture of it can be seen in Miedtank's books (Miedtank 2001, 2003). The underside of this plate is also decorated in a manner reminiscent of the underside of the Chinese plate in Fig. 59 from PEM. A very similar plate dating to ca. 1735 was offered for sale by the Auction House Bergmann in December 2002 and is shown in Fig. 60. Besides crossed swords, the mark on this plate includes the painter's initial "K", which is associated with the earliest Blue Onion pieces. A slightly later example from ca. 1740 is in the Syz Collection in the Smithsonian Institution and is shown in Fig. 61.

Fig. 60. Plate (Meissen, c. 1735) decorated in the three-fruit variant of the Blue Onion Pattern, D 8.65", crossed swords and painter's initial "K". A similar plate from the Dr. Carl Spitzner Collection is on display in the Dresden Porcelain Collection (*courtesy of Auktionshaus Bergmann, Erlangen, Germany*) (estimated value $3,500-4,500).

Fig. 61. Plate (Meissen c. 1740) decorated with the three-fruit variant of the Blue Onion Pattern, D 10" (*reproduced with permission, The Hans Syz Collection, Smithsonian Institution, Washington, DC USA*).

All of these early examples have borders trisected into symmetrical sections by the three fruits and are examples of a version of the Blue Onion pattern referred to as the three-fruit variant. This variant disappears around 1740 and does not reappear until late in the nineteenth century (under the pattern name "Original Blue Onion Pattern after Dr. Spitzner" or *Original Zwiebelmuster nach Dr. Spitzner*, cf. next chapter) in an attempt to reinvigorate the pattern. Around 1740 the number of fruits on the border is reduced to two. It is this two-fruit variant that has defined the pattern to this date. The earliest examples of the two-fruit variant also bear the painter's initial "K". It is for this reason that the painter "K" (Kretzschmar or more likely Kolmberger) is often considered to be the originator of the pattern. The two variants may have coexisted during the early 1740s. Several eighteenth century Blue Onion plates of the two-fruit variant are shown in Figs. 62-83 together with their marks and painter's initials to illustrate the variability of the pattern. The collector will find it worthwhile to carefully compare these early examples of the pattern.

On every example of Meissen's three-fruit variant the stems of the fruits point outwards, just like on the Chinese originals. The three "blessed fruits" will now be discussed in some detail since they vary appreciably with time and can sometimes be helpful in dating pieces.

Fig. 62. Dinner plate (Meissen, c. 1750), Blue Onion Pattern with all leaves on the peach having a common origin and a segmented "onion" on V-shaped stalk (see text for discussion of the fruits), D 9.25" (estimated value $400-600).

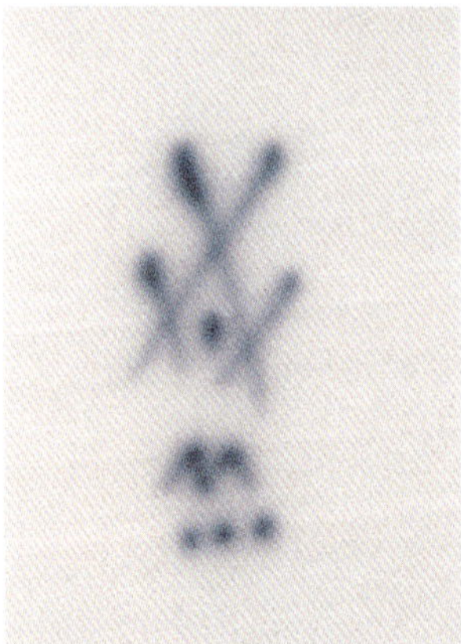

Left:
Fig. 63. Mark on plate of Fig. 62, crossed swords mark and painter's initial "M" over three dots in a row, attributed to Johann Gottfried Müller (active 1744-77), also impressed "32".

In the Chinese decorative arts the pomegranate is the symbol of fecundity and fathering male offspring. Pomegranates on Chinese originals are drawn in a naturalistic manner with a realistic shape, and displaying the remnants of the calyx. The pomegranate has also been used as a decorative element on Chinese export porcelain all by itself, not just in combination with the other fruits (Eberlein 1950). Pomegranates are usually shown as split open on one side, revealing their interior seed structure. The seeds are usually drawn as round circles, or sometimes, in greater detail with a pit and the surrounding flesh. The pomegranates on Meissen pieces are usually split open on both sides but the seeds still look natural. In the two-fruit variant some of the features of the pomegranate are transferred to the peach, while the pomegranate acquires aspects of the citrus fruit.

The peach symbolizes longevity. In the three-fruit variant it is drawn similar to the Chinese original. When the transition to the two-fruit variant occurred sometime during the 1740s the painters began to draw the peach as if it had an inner seed structure like the pomegranate. This practice became less common after 1750 but can be found sporadically until 1770 and was revived in the late nineteenth century. After about 1745 the seeds are often drawn as a crosshatched triangle. The simplified representation of the seeds by a crosshatched triangle after that date is by no means universal, as some scholars have implied (Miedtank 2001). The bowl in Fig. 78 with the painter's mark Mö attributed to Möbius (cf. Fig. 79) from ca. 1765 shows very clearly the more detailed structure of the seeds. Similarly, it is wrong to assert that the crosshatching is a later Meissen oversimplification of the more detailed original Chinese seed structure. The simplified motif can also be seen on the Chinese plate from the Peabody Essex Museum (cf. detail in Fig. 84).

Fig. 64. Dinner plate (Meissen, c. 1750), Blue Onion Pattern, the "onion" is not segmented and a stalk is indicated by two parallel lines, D 9.5" (estimated value $400-600).

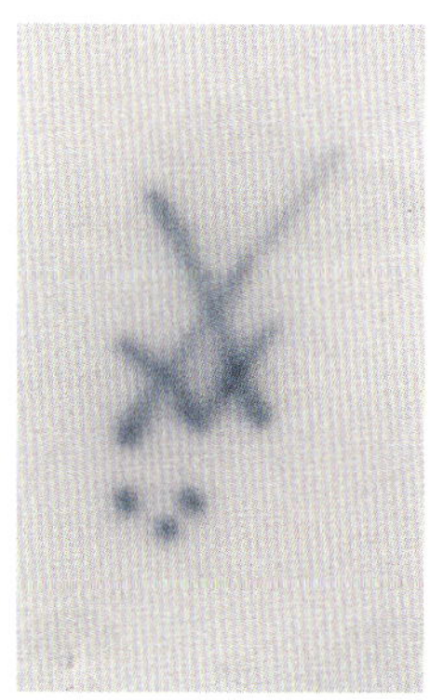

Fig. 65. Mark on plate of Fig. 64, crossed swords mark and painter's mark of three dots defining a triangle (cannot be attributed), also impressed "67".

The three (and sometimes four) leaves originating from its left side represent another telling characteristic of the peach. Up until ca. 1760 the three (or four) leaves have a common point of origin. This is shown in the detail of the plate by Möbius (cf. Figs. 66 and 67) in Fig. 85.

Fig. 66. Dinner plate (Meissen, c. 1765-74), Blue Onion Pattern, D 9.5" (estimated value $400-600).

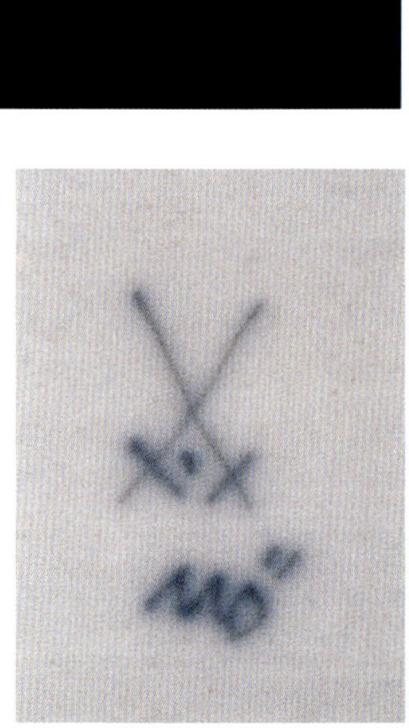

Fig. 67. Mark on plate of Fig. 66, crossed swords mark with dot and painter's initial Mö attributed to Johann Carl Möbius (Möbius, Sr. active 1763-80), also impressed "6".

After 1760 a different tradition sets in whereby the single leaf originates at a point below the others. This manner of drawing the leaves prevails throughout the nineteenth century and continues to this date. It is clear from the pictures, however, that both Möbius and the blue painter who marked his work with a circle have drawn the leaves in both traditions.

Another variant of the peach with all three leaves drawn attached to each other in a row is encountered during 1740-1760. It can be seen on the plate in Fig. 83 and also on an earlier plate from 1740 shown below in Fig. 86 with the border shown in greater detail in Fig. 87 and the mark in Fig. 88.

Fig. 68. Dinner plate (Meissen, c. 1740-60), Blue Onion Pattern, D 9.5" (estimated value $400-600).

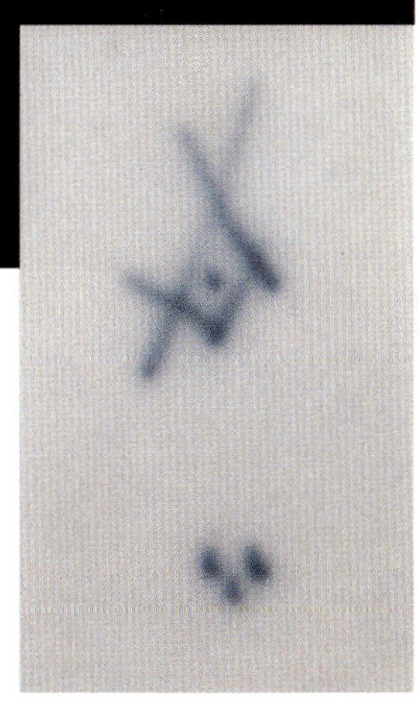

Fig. 69. Mark on plate of Fig. 68, crossed swords mark with dot and painter's mark of three dots defining a triangle (cannot be attributed), also impressed "94".

Fig. 70. Dinner plate (Meissen, c. 1750), Blue Onion Pattern, D 9.25" (estimated value $400-600).

Fig. 71. Mark on plate of Fig. 70, crossed swords mark with dot and painter's mark of a circle well above the swords (cannot be attributed) without other impressed or incised marks.

Fig. 72. Plate (Meissen, c. 1760-74), Blue Onion, D 9" (*courtesy of a private collection*).

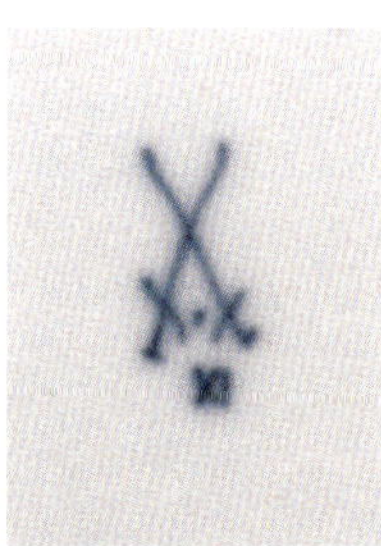

Fig. 73. Mark on plate of Fig. 72, crossed swords mark with dot and painter's mark "XI" rarely seen on ware predating the Marcolini period (cannot be attributed), also incised "+" and impressed "12".

Fig. 74. Plate (Meissen, c. 1750), Blue Onion, D 9" (*courtesy of a private collection*).

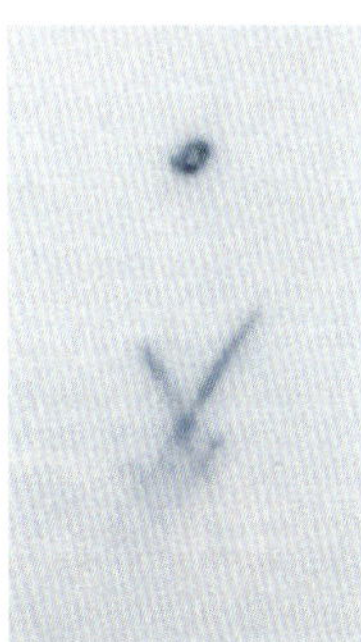

Fig. 75. Mark on plate of Fig. 74, crossed swords mark with painter's mark "O" well above the swords (cannot be attributed), also impressed "54".

Fig. 76. Plate (Meissen, c. 1765), Blue Onion, D 9" (*courtesy of a private collection*).

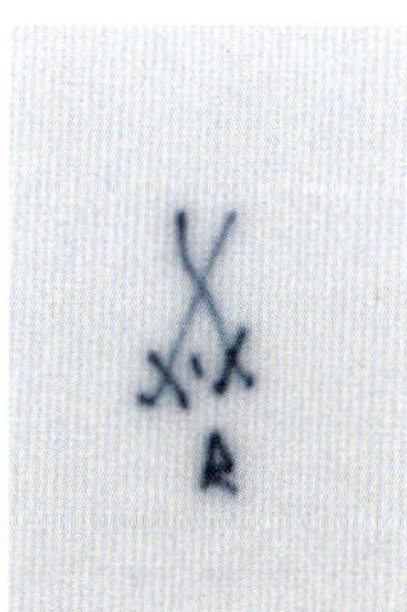

Fig. 77. Mark on plate of Fig. 76, crossed swords mark with painter's initial "R" attributed to Johann Heinrich Rudolf (active 1763-1777), also impressed "x" and "12".

Fig. 78. Bowl (Meissen, c. 1765-74), Blue Onion, D 9" (*courtesy of a private collection*).

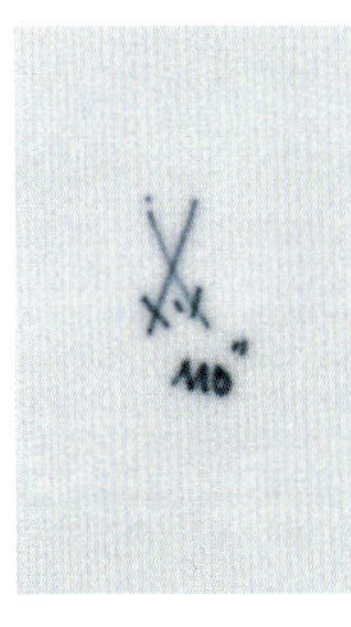

Fig. 79. Mark on plate of Fig. 78, crossed swords mark with painter's initial "Mö" attributed to Johann Carl Möbius (Möbius, Sr. active 1763-80).

Fig. 80. Reticulated plate (Meissen c. 1774-1814). Blue Onion, D 9" with continuous reticulation, marked with painter's numeral "2" and the crossed swords over star mark of the Marcolini period (*courtesy of the Doris P. Simonson Collection*).

Fig. 81. Plate (Meissen c. 1763-70), smooth rim, Blue Onion (*courtesy of the Doris P. Simonson Collection*).

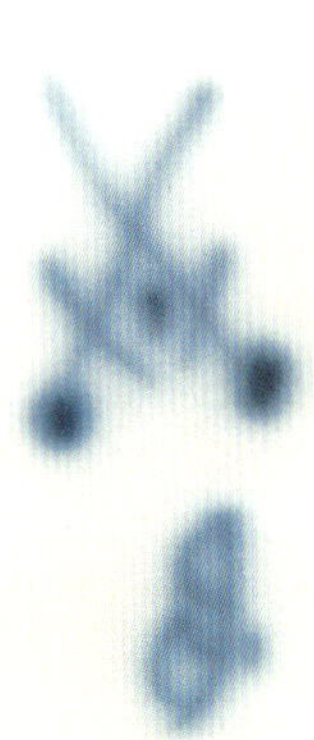

Fig. 82. Mark on plate of Fig. 81, crossed swords mark with painter's initial "J" in script possibly for Johann Michael Jancke (active since 1741, blue painter 1763-70).

Fig. 83. Dinner plate (Meissen, c. 1760) decorated in the two-fruit variant of the Blue Onion Pattern, D 8.75", crossed swords mark with painter's symbol of three dots shown in the insert (*courtesy of Auktionshaus Bergmann, Erlangen, Germany*) (estimated value $400-600).

Fig. 84. Detail of the pomegranate in Fig. 58 showing highly stylized rendering of its internal structure. Pieces like this from the royal collection served as models for the early blue painters (*reproduced with permission, Peabody Essex Museum, Salem MA*).

Fig. 85. Detail of the plate by Möbius in Fig. 66 showing a common origin for all leaves on the peach.

Fig. 86. Plate (most likely Meissen c. 1740). Blue Onion. D 9.13" (estimated value $400-600).

Fig. 87. Detail of plate in Fig. 86 showing the three leaves on the peach arranged sequentially and with serrated edges, in a manner ascribed to pre-1740 pieces.

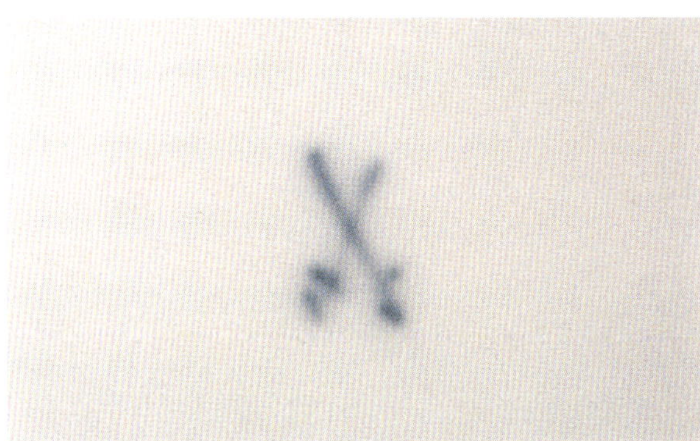

Fig. 88. Mark on plate of Fig. 86, attributed by Arnold (Arnold 1989) to c. 1740. Roentgen (Roentgen 1996) attributes the same mark and manner of drawing the peach to a 19th century Thuringian forgery.

The third fruit has been the subject of controversy. It is drawn with a segmented structure both on the Chinese originals as well as on Meissen porcelain. If one adheres to the three "blessed fruit" interpretation, then this fruit represents a citrus fruit, most likely a mandarin orange, the symbol of Buddha. The segmented structure has also been interpreted as representing the ribbed surface of a melon or pumpkin. Comparison with polychrome Chinese originals has lead to the suggestion it is most likely a pumpkin based on the color. Gourds in Chinese symbolism typically represent affluence and happiness.

In the two-fruit variant the segmented structure of this fruit appears to have been transposed to the pomegranate. The stylized calyx remnants of the pomegranate, together with the segmented structure borrowed from the mandarin orange (or gourd), gave rise to the idea of an "onion" and hence to the name Blue Onion. This is a misnomer that has lasted for over two centuries. Unlike the peach, the "onion" in the two-fruit variant is supported by two stalks, which either meet together forming a V shape or are parallel depending on the painter. Parallel stalks appear consistently in the work of the blue painter identified with a triple dot mark (cf. Figs. 64, 68, 83, and Fig. 183).

In the two-fruit variant the peaches and "onions" appear in pairs, with the double stems of the "onions" pointing towards the well of the plate and the peach stems pointing towards the rim. There are four such pairs separated by a very simple motif of leaves and flowers. This arrangement persists throughout the nineteenth and twentieth centuries and up to the present in the standard form of the Blue Onion pattern.

Ledge motifs: The ledge motifs are equally diverse. The ledge of the three-fruit variant is decorated with lotus flowers on an ornate blue background. Later examples have four non-descript flowers coinciding with the peach connected with wavy garlands. The sprigs of leaves on the garlands have been interpreted as pine needles (Sonntag 1999). The details of the garland varied from piece to piece until a much-simplified pattern arose in the nineteenth century.

Well motifs: The very busy design in the well of a Blue Onion plate is the best known part of this pattern. The design is suitable for the decoration of surfaces of arbitrary shape and size and is found on tureens, pitchers, tea, coffee, and chocolate pots and numerous other pieces of dinnerware. All the design elements of the well originate from the small patch of earth at the bottom center. A stem growing to the right terminates in the large chrysanthemum that dominates the pattern. The little dots around the flower are pollen grains coming out of the stamens drawn among the petals. Just below it there is a second flower, viewed from the side also a chrysanthemum, though it is sometimes drawn as a lotus blossom. Mixing and matching different flowers on the same branch is a known Far Eastern characteristic. A bamboo tree rises towards the left from the same patch of earth. Some sort of vine, conventionally accepted to be a morning glory, winds itself around the bamboo tree. A pair of leaves with serrated edges capped with a peony completes the pattern. A third leaf rising in the background can be found on some very early pre-1740 pieces. The leaves on early pieces are typically shaded in blue with the veins in white. The situation is reversed in newer pieces with the leaves essentially white and the veins in blue.

The flower and bamboo together represent the competing Chinese concepts of the yin and the yang and their balanced presentation in the pattern is symbolic of the complete human being.

Another form that harmonizes well with the Blue Onion pattern is the leaf-shaped sweetmeat dish shown in Fig. 89. This shape has remained popular to this date, however nineteenth century examples (like the one shown in Fig. 254 in the next chapter) are simpler in their decoration. They typically lack the applied flowers that grow out of the twig-shaped handle, as shown in the close up of Fig. 90.

Fig. 89. Leaf-shaped dish (Meissen, c. 1770) in the Blue Onion pattern, L 6.5", W 7" (estimated value $325-350).

Fig. 90. Detail of the handle for dish in Fig. 89 showing the applied flowers.

Fig. 91. Sugar caster (Meissen c. 1765), baluster shaped with reticulated screw-on top and acorn finial, H 6.25", decorated in the Blue Onion Pattern, attributed to Johann Michael Jancke (active since 1741, blue painter 1763-70), the peach drawn with the inner structure of a pomegranate (*courtesy of Auktionshaus Bergmann, Erlangen, Germany*), (estimated value $1,250-1,500).

So far we have discussed the eighteenth century Blue Onion pattern only in terms of plates, bowls, and platters. Examples of three-dimensional objects are the ca. 1745 sugar caster shown in Fig. 91 and the Marcoloni period pitcher from the last quarter of the eighteenth century with a mask ("mascarone") at the base of the spout (Fig. 92).

Fig. 92. Coffeepot without lid (Meissen c. 1775-1814), Blue Onion, H 5", with a mask of a bearded man at the base of the spout, Marcolini period crossed swords marks over star shown in the inset (*courtesy of Auktionshaus Bergmann, Erlangen, Germany*), (estimated value $1,000-1250).

A very significant piece is the footed basket of Fig. 93. The basket is supported by a figural pedestal of a boy and girl chasing each other around a tree stump. It is derived from a form originally modeled by Carl Christoph Punct that has served as an inspiration for the elegant "statuary for the table" so popular during the second half of the nineteenth century. Punct was hired as an assistant to Kaendler in 1761, but died of consumption shortly thereafter in 1765. Berling remarks that the figures of the original as modeled by Punct were later given more pleasing facial expressions by Kaendler. The basket in this example is solid and was probably intended for serving wet sweetmeats or sliced citrus fruits, typically lemons. The baskets of the nineteenth century variants that will be discussed in the next chapter are almost invariantly reticulated.

Fig. 93. Centerpiece (Meissen, c. 1770). Decorated with Indian Flowers and Insects on the outside and in the Blue Onion pattern inside. H 14". Blue painter's initial "M" over three dots defining a triangle, attributed to Johann Gottfried Müller (active 1744-77) (*courtesy of Auktionshaus Bergmann, Erlangen, Germany*), (estimated value $2,750-3,500).

The mark on the footed basket includes an "M" over three dots. This mark is associated with Johann Gottfried Müller (active 1744-77); the object is probably from c. 1770. The crossed swords mark with a dot between the hilts is also consistent with this dating. The interior of the footed bowl is decorated in the Blue Onion pattern; however, the boy and girl figures are clearly related to the corresponding tureen finials from the same period shown in Figs. 125-127 and decorated with German Flowers and Insects.

Another particularly noteworthy item is the oval box with cover from the Syz collection shown in Fig. 94. It belongs clearly to the "two-fruit" variant and the leaves are shaded in blue. The collection catalogue (Syz 1979) dates this piece to 1730-35. Based on its overall appearance it is very likely about ten years younger, dating to 1740-45.

Fig. 94. Footed container with lid (Meissen, c. 1730-45), Blue Onion with the peach drawn as having the internal structure of a pomegranate, H 3.63", L 6.5", crossed swords mark above two connected dots (*reproduced with permission, The Hans Syz Collection, Smithsonian Institution, Washington, DC USA*).

Eighteenth Century Blue Onion from Other Manufactories:

The Blue Onion pattern was not the most popular pattern during the eighteenth century. That distinction belonged to the Strawflower pattern that will be discussed later. Nevertheless, it was embraced quickly by other major manufactories, first by the Royal Porcelain Manufactory, Berlin (KPM) in 1770, followed by Ludwigsburg, and Royal Copenhagen in 1790. The KPM version of the Blue Onion pattern (cf. Fig. 95) appears much more uniform. A distinctive feature is the representation of the three leaves on the peach. In the KPM version all three leaves are directly attached to the fruit as shown in Fig. 96.

Fig. 95. Plate (Royal Porcelain Manufactory (KPM) Berlin, 1775-1800) decorated in the KPM adaptation of the Blue Onion Pattern (estimated value $200-300).

Fig. 96. Detail of the peach on the plate of Fig. 95, the three leaves originate independently, typical of 18th century KPM Blue Onion decoration.

Fig. 97. Plate (Chinese Kangxi Period c. 1700) decorated in underglaze blue with several Far Eastern motifs like rock, peony, prunus, vase, etc., D 10" (estimated value $200-300).

The Rock and Bird Pattern (*Fels- und Vogeldekor*) and Related Avian Designs:

The combination of peonies, rocks and bamboo, and birds in flight are familiar motifs from Far Eastern paintings, porcelain, and textiles. These design elements were quickly adopted by the Meissen Manufactory during the first half of the eighteenth century. The motifs were masterfully integrated into a family of patterns, the best known being the so-called Rock and Bird (*Fels- und Vogeldekor*) pattern. The pattern was introduced in 1725 and shows quite a bit of variability in its execution.

The central motif of this pattern is a highly stylized rock. The rock derives from Chinese blue and white originals of the Kangxi period, an example of which is given in Fig. 97. Rocks are an important Chinese art form. Convoluted T'ai Lake limestone rocks were favored decorative three-dimensional objects (*tai-hu* garden stones) that have inspired rock portraits by Chinese artists like the painter Lan Ying (1585-1664), whose work can be seen in the Minneapolis Institute of Arts. The Chinese rocks are typically more elaborate and show the details of their convoluted structures, a feature seldom seen on Meissen designs. The rocks on the Meissen and related European blue and white renditions of this pattern are irregular polygons shaded in blue, with some exceptions, as on the teapot of Fig. 98. To the left of the rock is a scraggly twig terminating in a single leaf, accompanied by a swarm of star-like structures. According to one interpretation cited by von Barsewisch (von Barsewisch 1988), these stars represent the remains of bamboo branches. To the right of the rock we see the branch of a plum tree (*Prunus*), a symbol of resilience and fortitude. A bird in flight with its head facing backwards completes the pattern. The drawing of the bird on the original Oriental pieces is quite elaborate and is thought to represent a pheasant. On eighteenth century European examples the bird is highly stylized but nevertheless esthetically pleasing.

The teapot with a so-called "J-handle" decorated in the Rock and Bird pattern is shown in Figs. 98 and 99. It is marked with the blue painter's initial "H" under the crossed swords at the base of the handle rather than on the underside. This location for the mark is generally quite unusual but encountered rather often in J-handled teapots.

Fig. 98. Teapot (Meissen c 1740-45) with a "J" handle decorated in the Rock and Bird pattern, H 4", L (handle-to-spout) 6.5" (estimated value as is $300, mint with original lid $900-1,100).

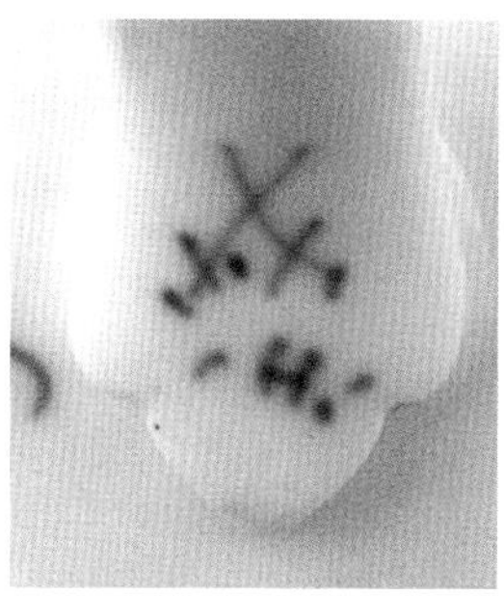

Fig. 99. Mark on teapot of Fig. 98, crossed swords over painter's initial "H" and dots, cannot be attributed.

A coffee pot in the Rock and Bird pattern from the second half of the eighteenth century is shown in Fig. 100. It has been painted by the blue painter initialing with three dots. The initial is at the foot rim, rather than under the swords.

Fig. 100. Coffeepot (Meissen, c. 1750-1775), Rock and Bird pattern, H 7.13", noticeably restored, crossed swords mark and painter's mark of three dots at the foot rim (*courtesy of Auktionshaus Bergmann, Erlangen, Germany*), (estimated value as is $400-600, mint $900-1200).

The popularity of this pattern waned during the second half of the eighteenth century and was produced only sporadically by Meissen. Other manufactories, specifically the Royal Vienna Manufactory, continued high production volumes however. A factory overdecorated coffeepot by Royal Vienna and dated 1805 is shown in Fig. 101. The pot is decorated with the Viennese version of Rock and Bird in underglaze blue and is further enhanced by overglaze decoration in red and gold. This piece is believed to be factory-decorated. We will have more to say about overdecorated pieces in the final sections of this chapter.The Viennese pieces are usually decorated with more luscious foliage and the quality of the painting is very high. Early nineteenth century Meissen examples became much cruder. The bird is drawn more like a round bowl to which feathers and feet have been haphazardly attached. This can be seen in the diminutive mid-nineteenth century Meissen quatrefoil cup and saucer shown in Figs. 102 and 103. The close up of the cup in Fig. 104 illustrates the point. The rendition of this pattern in underglaze green on a plate from ca. 1820 is also much less refined.

Fig. 101. Coffeepot (Royal Porcelain Manufactory Vienna, 1808). Rock and Bird pattern overdecorated in the Manufactory with gold highlights and rust red flowers and foliage, the finial further painted in yellow and copper green. H 7.5", L (spout-to-handle) 5" (estimated value $500-750).

Fig. 102. Demitasse and saucer (Meissen c. 1880), rare diminutive quatrefoil shape decorated in the Rock and Bird pattern. Cup: L 2.5", W 2", H 1.38"; Saucer: L 3.75", W 3" (estimated value $300).

Fig. 103. Detail of saucer shown in Fig. 102. Note the depression in the well of the cup is sometimes absent in older shapes. Bird highly stylized and rather crude compared to examples from the 18th century.

Fig. 104. Detail of cup shown in Fig. 102.

Numerous other variants with avian patterns have been recognized by von Barsewisch (von Barsewisch 1988), depicting a phoenix or water birds together with peonies and *prunus* branches. A stein with waterfowl from ca. 1730-1740 from the von Barsewisch collection is shown in Figs. 105 and 106. A particularly impressive reticulated basket from 1740, also from the von Barsewisch collection, can be seen in Figs. 107 and 108. The basket stands on four elaborately modeled paw feet. The interior depicts a phoenix surrounded by a plum tree (*prunus*). The inspiration for the phoenix motif comes from a mythical Chinese bird, the *feng-huang* (Sonntag 1999). The Bird Pattern (*Vogelmodell*), depicting a bird perched on a hedge of peonies with a rock, is closely related to the Rock and Bird pattern. An early and very carefully painted example is the square bowl of Fig. 109.

Fig. 105. Tankard (Meissen, c. 1730-40) decorated with waterfowl over wetlands, crossed swords mark with "O", H 5.75", D 5" (*Courtesy of the Dr. B. von Barsewisch Collection/Schlossmuseum Wolfshagen Prignitz*).

Fig. 106. Another view of the tankard in Fig. 105 (*Courtesy of the Dr. B. von Barsewisch Collection/ Schlossmuseum Wolfshagen Prignitz*).

Fig. 107. Reticulated basket (Meissen, c. 1730-40) with an unusual reticulation pattern, and applied flowers on four claw feet. Crossed swords mark with lozenge-shaped "O" above. H 4", D 8" (Courtesy of the Dr. B. von Barsewisch Collection/Schlossmuseum Wolfshagen Prignitz).

Fig. 108. Interior decoration of the basket in Fig. 107 showing a phoenix on prunus branch (Courtesy of the Dr. B. von Barsewisch Collection/Schlossmuseum Wolfshagen Prignitz).

Fig. 109. Square bowl (Meissen, c. 1740) decorated in the Rock and Bird pattern with bird perched on a hedge of peonies, crossed swords over vertical line, L 10.75", W 7.75" (*Courtesy of the Dr. B. von Barsewisch Collection/ Schlossmuseum Wolfshagen Prignitz*).

Japanese-inspired Designs and Patterns:

The importation of porcelain from China was interrupted during the middle of the seventeenth century, first during the popular uprising against the Ming dynasty and then the ensuing national resistance to the foreign (Tartar) Manchu rulers. We already saw in the previous section how these events benefited the blue faience production in Delft. The interruption of Chinese porcelain importation also gave Japanese porcelain manufactories the opportunity to gain a foothold in the European market, and influence Western tastes. The completion of partial underglaze blue decoration with additional overglaze red and gold details, as in the restrained Kakiemon or more flamboyant Imari designs, had an impact on Meissen's artists. We have already seen in Fig. 26 a rare and extremely well executed example by Horn, integrating over and under the glaze decoration. A somewhat more widely produced pattern is composed of underglaze blue floral motifs with reserves decorated with crayfish. This is the so-called Lobster pattern (*Hummernmuster*), and an example of it from the Syz collection (Syz 1979) is shown in Fig. 110.

Fig. 110. Plate (Meissen, c. 1730-35) from the Hans Syz Collection, the underglaze blue foliate decoration of the well is derived from the Indian Flower pattern and is surrounded by crayfish painted overglaze in blue, rust red, orange, grass-green, sea-green, gold, and black within reserves in the ledge (cavetto), D 8.63", crossed swords mark over painter's initial "K" (*reproduced with permission, The Smithsonian Institution, Washington, D.C. USA*).

The crayfish motif has also been copied on European tin glazed earthenware. An example is a large round platter in the Toledo Museum of Art, attributed to the Guillibaud factory in Rouen, France, and roughly contemporaneous with the Meissen example from the Syz collection.

Two other Kakiemon inspired objects by Meissen and by the Vienna Manufactory, both currently in the von Barsewisch collection, are shown in Figs. 111-113.

Fig. 111. Plate (Meissen, c. 1730-40), Imari inspired decoration with an underglaze blue chrysanthemum embellished with overglaze rust-red painting, crossed swords over "S", D 8.75" (*Courtesy of the Dr. B. von Barsewisch Collection/ Schlossmuseum Wolfshagen Prignitz*).

Fig. 112. Deep plate (Royal Vienna mid-18th century). Imari inspired decoration with an underglaze blue vase and leaves and overglaze rust red flowers. D 9.5" (*Courtesy of the Dr. B. von Barsewisch Collection/Schlossmuseum Wolfshagen Prignitz*).

Fig. 113. Underside of plate shown in Fig. 112 (*Courtesy of the Dr. B. von Barsewisch Collection/Schlossmuseum Wolfshagen Prignitz*).

The most popular product of the Japanese artistic influence is a very Imari-like pattern known as *Tischchenmuster*. The word literally means "small table pattern" in German, and when properly pronounced has a pleasing cadence to it. It is difficult to invent a mellifluous English term for the name of this pattern. It has also been translated as the Japanese Garden with Table Pattern. The pattern, which combines a basic underglaze blue design completed with overglaze polychrome floral decoration, was introduced in 1732 and has been in continuous production without significant modifications to this date. According to Sterba (Sterba 1989), only the underglaze blue portion of the pattern is of Japanese origin, the polychrome flowers being typical of Meissen's own version of Indian flowers (*indianische Blumen*).

Details of just the unfinished blue underglaze design are shown in Fig. 114 on a c. 1740 covered creamer from the von Barsewisch collection. The blue part of the pattern consists of leaves and branches that become part of the floral polychrome painting. More interesting is the stylized small table supported by two "X" frames. It most likely derives from the Imari "table in landscape" motif. In the latter, however the table is drawn in greater detail.

Fig. 114. Small lidded pot on claw feet and acanthus leaf relief under the spout (Meissen, c. 1740). Incomplete *Tischchenmuster* showing only the underglaze blue part. H 5", D 3" at the top (*Courtesy of the Dr. B. von Barsewisch Collection/Schlossmuseum Wolfshagen Prignitz*).

An extensive collection of fully decorated nineteenth century *Tischchenmuster* shapes will be shown in the next chapter.

Another stunning example of this genre not depicted here can be seen in the Meissen Manufactory Museum. It is a 9 1/2" plate with a vase and foliage painted in underglaze blue completed with flowers painted in red over the glaze (see Figure 91 in Sonntag 1999 or Figure 31 in Karpinski 2001).

The Strawflower Pattern (*Strohblumendekor*):

Today this particular pattern is widely associated with tableware by Royal Copenhagen. The reader will immediately recognize it in Figs. 121-123. In fact the Strawflower pattern originated with the Meissen Manufactory, and during the second half of the eighteenth century it and not the Blue Onion was Meissen's most popular pattern on tableware meant for everyday use by the middle class.

The pattern consists of the central flower, a chrysanthemum viewed from the side, surrounded by four segments with a flower with six petals, presumably a peony, and foliage (von Barsewisch 1988). This pattern emerged from the continuous simplification of various Indian flower patterns. The earliest example of this pattern is a cup dated 1740 with German flowers painted in puce on the interior and the strawflower decoration in underglaze blue on the exterior (cf. Arnold 1989). A snuffbox from 1750, elaborately decorated with a painting of a lady's boudoir, contains representations of tableware in the Strawflower pattern. The Wegely factory, precursor of the Gotzkowsky and KPM Berlin, produced carefully copied imitations of the pattern during 1752-1757. It is listed in the *Preiscourante* of 1765, Meissen's price list. Several detailed pictures of a cup and saucer from ca. 1750-60 are shown in Figs. 115-118, together with the marks that convey a fairly complete impression of this pattern.

Fig. 116. Interior of cup shown in Fig. 115 showing the central flower in the plate well repeated on the inside of the cup.

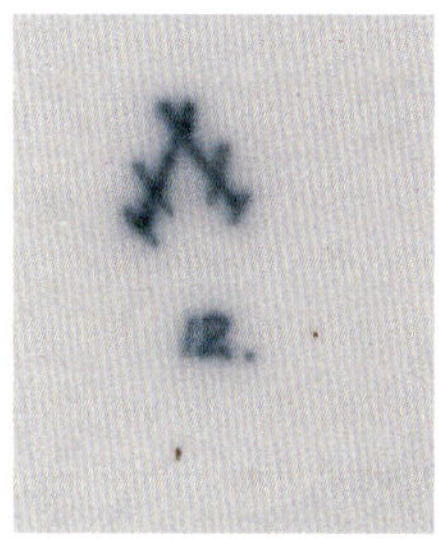

Fig. 117. Mark on the saucer of Fig. 115.

Fig. 118. Mark on the cup of Fig. 115.

Fig. 115. Cup and Saucer (Meissen, c. 1760) with ribbed relief molding in the Strawflower pattern, cup H 2", saucer D 5.38" (estimated value $250-350).

A somewhat later platter in this pattern from the Marcolini period (1774-1814) is shown in Fig. 119. It is 13.38" in length and has quatrefoil shape.

Fig. 119. Platter (Meissen, c. 1775-1780), fluted relief molding, Strawflower pattern, L 13.38", blue crossed swords mark with star over painter's initial "K" shown in inset (*courtesy of Auktionshaus Bergmann, Erlangen, Germany*), (estimated value $125-250).

The pattern is found almost exclusively on relief decoration known as ribbed or fluted (*gebrochener Stab*). This is not an optimal background for porcelain painting since the blue pigment tends to pool on the corrugated surface. The pattern is also very rustic and really does not suit Meissen's image in terms of quality and sophistication. The main motivation for its development was probably the low production cost. The pattern has been progressively simplified by the fifty or more manufactories that imitated it.

Among the many imitators were the Thuringian factories that blossomed during the later decades of the eighteenth century. An example probably from the Volkstedt manufactory bearing an imitation Meissen mark (cf. Fig. 356) is the teapot from ca. 1770 with sterling mounts, shown in Fig. 120. The design is already somewhat simplified and painted casually, and more telling especially when ambiguous marks are at issue, the quality of the glaze is visibly poor.

Fig. 120. Teapot with sterling mounts (Volkstedt? c. 1775) with "J" handle, Strawflower pattern most likely of Thuringian origin with false crossed swords marks, glaze and painting defects, H 4.5", L 7.5" (spout-to-handle) (*courtesy of Auktionshaus Bergmann, Erlangen, Germany*), (estimated value $300-400).

The Royal Copenhagen factory produced particularly felicitous versions of the pattern since the last quarter of the eighteenth century. By the end of the nineteenth century the pattern had come to be associated with Denmark. Dinnerware in this pattern became the hallmark of Copenhagen City Hall receptions. Figs. 121-123 show nineteenth and early twentieth century Royal Copenhagen versions of the pattern and, by comparison to the previous figures, demonstrate its modernization.

Fig. 121. Plate (Royal Copenhagen, c. 1894-98), late 19th century rendition of the Strawflower pattern on Royal Copenhagen porcelain (estimated value $25-50).

Fig. 122. Leaf-shaped dish (Royal Copenhagen, c. 1898-1923), 19th-20th century rendition of the Strawflower pattern on Royal Copenhagen porcelain (estimated value $150-175).

Fig. 123. Pair of double candelabra (Royal Copenhagen, c. 1969-74), late 20th century rendition of the Strawflower pattern on Royal Copenhagen porcelain, partially reticulated fluted body, H 10", mark shown in insert with bar under the letter "G" dating the piece to 1969-74 (courtesy of *Auktionshaus Bergmann, Erlangen, Germany*), (estimated value $900-1,100).

Two other Oriental motifs not shown here are the precursor of the Thistle Pattern (*Distelmuster*) and the Willow Pattern (*Felsen mit Trauerweide*) from ca. 1780.

European Floral Motifs: German Flowers and Insects *(Deutsche Blumen und Insekten)*:

Bouquets of flowers together with insects and sprigs of smaller individual flowers first appear in underglaze blue around 1740. European floral decorations differ in many ways from those inspired by the Far East. The highly stylized Far Eastern or Indian Flowers motifs are drawn in a manner reminiscent of the graphic arts. German flowers are painted with broad brushstrokes in the tradition of European painting. They are realistic in appearance and can be readily identified. The most popular flowers are roses, tulips, irises or anemones. The insects are butterflies, moths, or sometimes, fantasy insects with elongated bodies. This pattern reached its refined expression around 1745 on the decoration of a set for the Royal Court Confectionary in Warsaw modeled by Kaendler. The set is initialed by "AR" in script (for *Augustus Rex*) and is marked with the inventory mark K.H.C.W. (cf. Fig. 349). A plate from this set is shown in Fig. 124.

Fig. 124. Large plate of royal provenance (Meissen, c. 1745) decorated with German Flowers and Insects and bearing the monogram AR for *Augustus Rex*, the royal insignia of King August the Strong, crossed swords over blue painter's mark shown in Fig. 349. D 15" (*Courtesy of the Dr. B. von Barsewisch Collection/Schlossmuseum Wolfshagen Prignitz*).

Another impressive example of the German Flowers and Insects pattern is the pair of covered tureens with matching figural finials from ca. 1770. The figures are those of a boy and a girl facing each other. The female figure is easily recognized by the way she ties her hair in a bun. Details are shown in Figs. 125, 126, and 127. Figural finials with a girl or boy presenting a horn-of-plenty (cornucopia) are quite common on nineteenth century Blue Onion tureens but rare during the eighteenth century. Even more unusual are matching pairs of finials with figures facing each other. The pair of tureens together with the centerpiece of Fig. 93 represent some of the rare underglaze blue examples of "statuary for the table," a concept we encountered in our discussion of the dining traditions of the Saxon court and were the work of significant Meissen modelers. It is believed that the figural finials were modeled by Johann Friedrich Eberlein, the figural centerpiece, as mentioned earlier, by Punct.

Fig. 125. Covered tureen with figural finial and underplate (Meissen, c. 1770) decorated with German Flowers and Insects. Tureen internal dimensions, 7.5" by 5", H 7", underplate 13.75" by 9" (*Courtesy of the Dr. B. von Barsewisch Collection/Schlossmuseum Wolfshagen Prignitz*).

Fig. 126. Detail of the finial in Fig. 125 showing little boy gazing to his left and holding the mouth of the horn-of-plenty with his right hand (*Courtesy of the Dr. B. von Barsewisch Collection/Schlossmuseum Wolfshagen Prignitz*).

Fig. 127. Detail of the finial in a figural tureen, companion piece of Fig. 125 showing little girl gazing to her right and holding the mouth of the horn-of-plenty with her left hand (*Courtesy of the Dr. B. von Barsewisch Collection/Schlossmuseum Wolfshagen Prignitz*).

The boy and girl always strike the same pose on eighteenth and nineteenth century and later pulls. The girl holds the mouth of the horn-of-plenty with her left hand; the boy holds it always with his right.

Further typical examples of this pattern are the mid-eighteenth century coffeepot with a mask on the spout shown in Fig. 128 and the double leaf dish of Fig. 129. The shape of the former is the same as that of the coffee pot of Fig. 92 in the Blue Onion pattern.

Fig. 128. Coffeepot (Meissen, c. 1745-50) with relief mask of bearded man at the base of the spout, H 6.25", crossed swords mark and painter's mark "·/·" in underglaze blue shown in the inset (*courtesy of Auktionshaus Bergmann, Erlangen, Germany*), (estimated value $1,300-1,600).

Fig. 129. Double-leaf dish (Meissen, c. 1760) with molded leaf veins, decorated with German Flowers and Insects. L 10.5", W 7" (estimated value $300-400).

The German Flowers pattern has retained its popularity to this date and more nineteenth century examples will be shown in the next chapter.

Simple Floral Decorations:

The waning decades of the eighteenth century witnessed a declining interest in Far Eastern designs. Driven in part by worsening economic conditions, blue and white painting shifted to simple floral motives that were easy to draw, quick to apply, and therefore inexpensive to produce, all at the expense of artistic excellence. Nevertheless, the resulting, primarily utilitarian objects are still quite charming and have a place in every serious collection. Of the many simple floral patterns, three commonly encountered ones are shown here. They are the Wreath pattern (*Blumenkranz*) (shown in Figs. 130 and 131), the Little Blue Flowers pattern (*Blaublümchendekor*) from 1750 in Fig. 132 and the Leafy Border (*Blätterkante*) of Figs. 133 and 134 from the late Marcolini period, ca. 1810. Other patterns mentioned in the price lists are Garlands and Festoons.

Fig. 130. Sugar caster (Meissen, mid-18th century) Indian Flower decoration, underglaze blue crossed swords over the number "8". H 6.5" (*Courtesy of the Dr. B. von Barsewisch Collection/Schlossmuseum Wolfshagen Prignitz*).

Fig. 131. Cylindrical cup and saucer (Meissen 1775-1814), underglaze blue Wreath pattern, Marcolini period crossed swords mark over star shown in insert. (*courtesy of Auktionshaus Bergmann, Erlangen, Germany*). (estimated value $100-150).

Fig. 132. Three tea bowls and saucers (Meissen, c. 1750), Little Blue Flowers pattern on body with fluted relief molding, crossed swords mark shown in insert (*courtesy of Auktionshaus Bergmann, Erlangen, Germany*), (estimated value $1,000-1,500).

Fig. 133. Jug (Meissen, 1804-1817). Leafy Border pattern (*Blätterkantenmuster*), H 5.5", W 5.5" (estimated value $80-125).

Fig. 134. Blue underglaze crossed swords mark with star on jug in Fig. 37. Blue painter's mark 11, impressed numbers 14, 61, and letter B (on tableware to be painted blue 1804-1817).

Putti as Frolicking Children (*Kinder a la Raphael*):

A rather unusual, late eighteenth century motif, inspired by the work of the seventeenth century French artist Jacques Stella, is that of putti represented as frolicking children engaged in various games. This pattern is often referred to as "children in the manner of Raphael" (*Kinder a la Raphael*), though the style has nothing to do with Raphaelite painting. It refers to the cursory resemblance of the putti to a famous painting of an angel painted by Raphael in 1512 and held by the Dresden Art Collection (Gemäldegalerie Dresden Alte Meister). I prefer the designation "Frolicking Children." Tableware decorated in this manner were introduced around 1765, and are listed in the 1765 *Preiß-Courante*, the price list of the Meissen Manufactory, as "*spielende Kinder a la Raphael*". They did not attain the level of popularity their creators had hoped for, and were withdrawn from the market around 1800. They are no longer listed in the *Preiß-Courante* of 1799.

Jacques Stella, a French draftsman, painter, and printmaker was born in Lyon in 1596 and died in Paris in 1657. His father, Francois, a painter and art dealer, was of Flemish origin. From 1619 to 1622, Stella lived in Florence working for Cosimo II de Medici. In 1623 he moved to Rome, where he was influenced by the classicism of Nicolas Poussin's art. In 1634 Stella traveled to Venice, Milan, and Lyon before settling in Paris in 1635. With the help of Cardinal Richelieu he was appointed a royal painter (*premier peintre du roi*), and later also worked in Rouen and Versailles. Stella's series of drawings "*Les jeaux et plaisir de l'enfance*" ("The Games and Pastimes of Childhood") is a major source of the history of children's games. This series was converted to engravings by his niece Claudine Bouzonnet (1636-1697) and published in 1657 (Fig. 135).

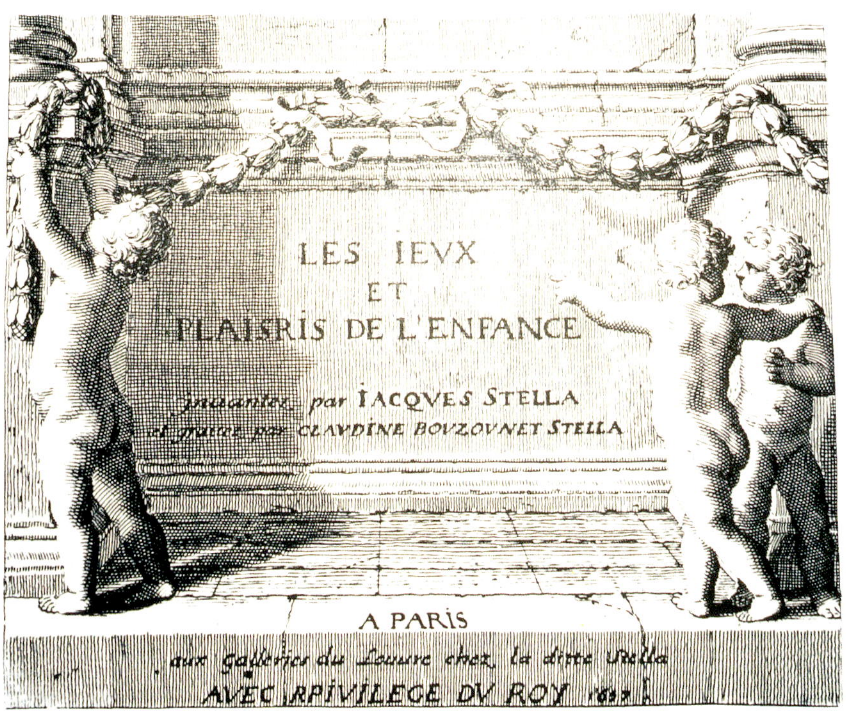

Fig. 135. Title page of "*Les Jeaux et Plaisirs de l' Enfance*" (Games and Pastimes of Childhood), drawings by Jacques Stella, engraved by Claudine Bouzonnet Stella, and published in 1657. Notice the misspelling of the word *plaisirs* as *plaisris* in the engraving.

Fig. 136. Round platter showing two putti playing field hockey from the pattern "Putti as frolicking children" (Meissen, 1765- 1770). D 13", painter's initial "L". Based in part on an engraving by Stella shown in Fig. 137 (*Courtesy of the Dr. B. von Barsewisch Collection/Schlossmuseum Wolfshagen Prignitz, Germany*).

The motif of "Frolicking Children" is probably one of Meissen's earliest, albeit unsuccessful, attempts to move beyond the declining tastes of the Rococo and adapt to the rising popularity of classicism. Christian Wilhelm Ernst Dietrich, brought in as director of painting in 1764, strongly encouraged development in this direction.

Examples of the motif are rare and do not come to market very often. The most common painter's initials associated with this pattern are "L" for David Benjamin Lindner (active 1764-1776) and "P" likely for Gottfried Prasser (active 1744-1777). The known examples in this pattern are mostly flat and deep plates, platters, and underplates. The tea caddy in Fig. 147 is quite unusual in this respect. One should differentiate between the designs copied directly from the engravings and those that are merely in the manner of Stella. We will first survey the pieces that have been copied directly and compare them to the original engravings. Most of the paintings on porcelain reproduce only portions of the original engravings, usually depicting only a single figure. A relatively rare painting of two putti is shown in Fig. 136. The putti are engaged in an early version of lacrosse or field hockey. The full engraving is shown in Fig. 137.

Fig. 137. La Crosse, illustration by Jacques Stella, engraved by Claudine Bouzonnet Stella (1657). Source of the Meissen decoration in Fig. 136.

Several plates with decorations copied directly from the engravings together with the original artwork are shown in Figs. 138-146.

Fig. 138. Soup bowl showing putto with jumping hoop from the pattern "Putti as frolicking children" (Meissen, 1765-1770). D 9". Based in part on an engraving by Stella shown in Fig. 139 (*Courtesy of the Dr. B. von Barsewisch Collection/Schlossmuseum Wolfshagen Prignitz, Germany*).

Fig. 140. Soup bowl showing baby putto in walker chasing a butterfly from the pattern "Putti as frolicking children" (Meissen, 1765-1770). D 9.5", painter's initial "P". Based in part on an engraving by Stella shown in Fig. 141 (*Courtesy of the Dr. B. von Barsewisch Collection/Schlossmuseum Wolfshagen Prignitz, Germany*).

Fig. 139. The Jumping Hoop and the Cup-and-Ball, illustration by Jacques Stella, engraved by Claudine Bouzonnet Stella (1657). Source of the Meissen decoration in Fig. 138.

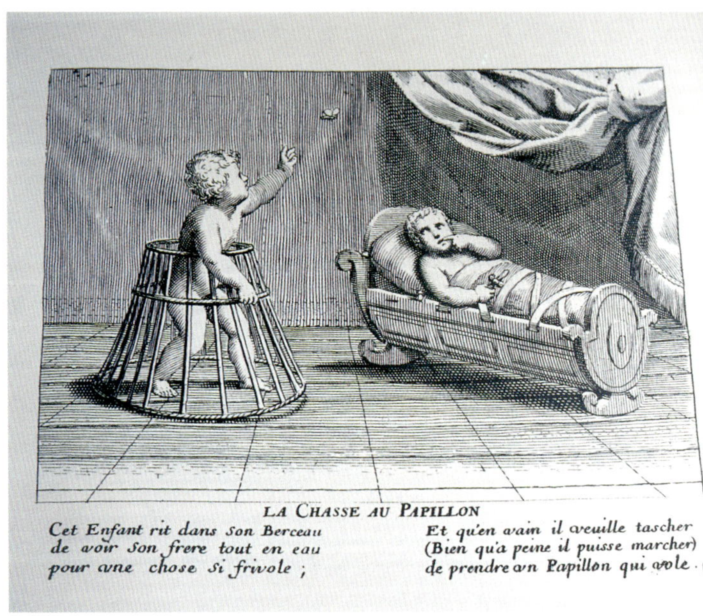

Fig. 141. Chasing Butterflies, illustration by Jacques Stella, engraved by Claudine Bouzonnet Stella (1657). Source of the Meissen decoration in Fig. 140.

Fig. 176. Tea bowl and saucer (Meissen c. 1750), underglaze blue Indian Flowers pattern later overdecorated with gold highlights and German Flowers in purple camaieu by an outside *Hausmaler*, bowl H 1.75", saucer D 5.13", crossed swords mark with painter's mark of an elongated circle or "." between the blades, mark shown in insert, (*courtesy of Auktionshaus Bergmann, Erlangen, Germany*), (estimated value $1500-1750).

Let us now turn our attention to outside decorations not attributable to a particular workshop. An exceptionally good example is the mid-eighteenth century tea bowl and saucer in the Indian Flowers pattern (Fig. 176). The underglaze blue pattern is carefully highlighted with gold and further enhanced with German flowers in purple camaieu.

The Meissen tea bowl and saucer of Fig. 176 are not factory overdecorated. This is evident from the fact that the decoration is not in the Meissen manner. An ambiguity arises only when the decoration imitates closely Meissen techniques. Meissen overdecoration consists of gold highlights of the underglaze blue design and polychrome floral additions in harmony with the underlying pattern. Such pieces are rare. As a general rule most of eighteenth century blue and white Meissen porcelain with polychrome embellishments was painted by mediocre artists outside the manufactory sometime during the nineteenth century. In the absence of provenance, however, it is extremely difficult to pass judgment on individual pieces. The following several examples may help illustrate the point. The overdecoration on the double-leaf dish (Fig. 177) in the Strawflower pattern from ca. 1763-1774 is very restrained and sympathetic to the underlying pattern. This piece may have been decorated in Meissen. Nevertheless in the absence of other evidence one has to err on the side of caution and still classify it as outside decoration.

Fig. 177. Double leaf dish (Meissen, c. 1765) molded relief showing leaf veins, Strawflower decoration, L 10.25", overdecorated outside the Manufactory with gold highlights and further embellished with iron red foliage (*courtesy of Auktionshaus Bergmann, Erlangen, Germany*), (estimated value $250-350).

Less restrained colors like the deep purples of Figs. 178-181 and careless painting like the haphazard shading in green and purple are clear indications of nineteenth century outside decoration by "botchers."

Fig. 178. Cup and saucer (Meissen, c.1760-70), Blue Onion with later unrestrained overdecoration by *Pfutscher* during the 19th century (*courtesy of a private collection*).

Fig. 179. Plate (Meissen, c. 1775-1814) decorated with the Blue Onion pattern during the Marcolini period with later intensely polychrome overdecoration outside the Meissen Manufactory (*courtesy of the Doris P. Simonson Collection*).

Fig. 180. Marcolini period crossed swords over star on the plate of Fig. 179. Note painter's initial "L" near foot rim (*courtesy of the Doris P. Simonson Collection*).

Fig. 181. Plate (Meissen, c. 1750), with continuous reticulation, Blue Onion pattern with later intensely polychrome overdecoration outside the Meissen Manufactory (*courtesy of the Doris P. Simonson Collection*).

Particularly interesting is the comparison of the two overdecorated Blue Onion bowls shown (together with their marks and design details) in Figs. 182-187. They were probably decorated by the same artist or at least in the same workshop. Yet one of them (Fig. 182) is a Meissen piece from the second half of the eighteenth century, the other (Fig. 185) by KPM from around 1800-1810. Clearly both pieces have received their overdecoration at the same decorating shop outside their respective manufactories, possibly decades after they were first sold.

Fig. 182. Soup bowl (Meissen, c. 1750), Blue Onion, with 19th century overdecoration outside the Meissen Manufactory, D 9", H 1.5" (estimated value $250-350).

Fig. 183. Detail of the bowl in Fig. 182 showing the copper green and iron red enamel colors used overglaze, also note the leaves on the side of the peach have a common origin consistent with the imputed date of manufacture.

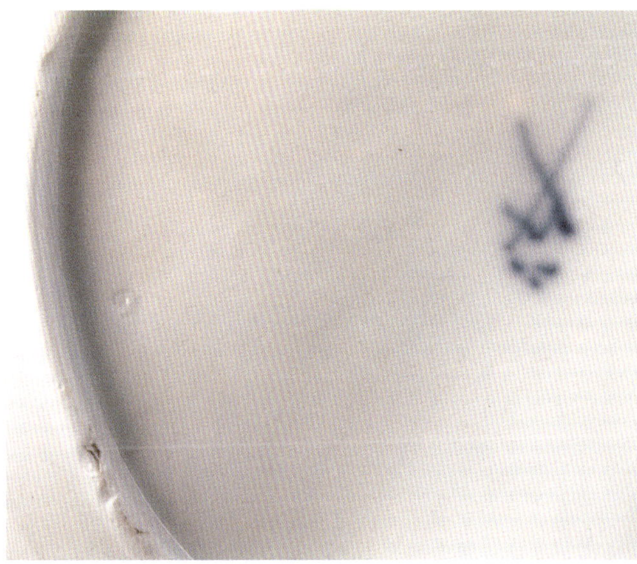

Fig. 184. Mark on bowl of Fig. 182, incised number "6" crossed swords over three dots defining a triangle.

Fig. 185. Soup bowl (KPM Berlin, c. 1780), KPM's version of the Blue Onion pattern with 19th century outside overdecoration strikingly similar to that of the bowl in Fig. 182, possibly from the same workshop, D 8.88", H 2" (estimated value $200-300).

Fig. 186. Edge decoration of the soup bowl in Fig. 185, the three leaves on the peach are attached individually, a distinguishing feature of the KPM Blue Onion pattern.

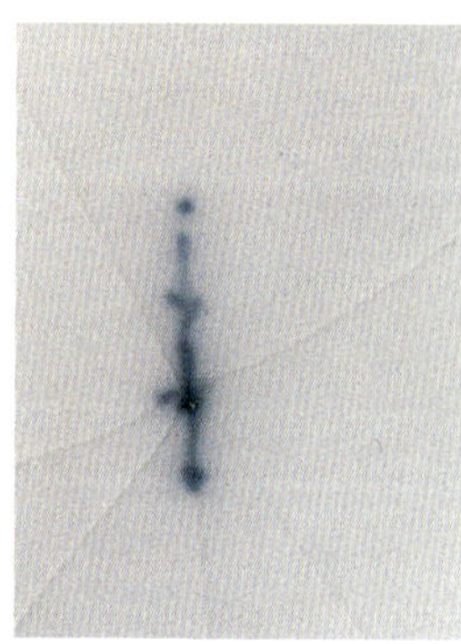

Fig. 187. Mark on the bowl of Fig. 185, showing the 18th century underglaze blue scepter mark.

The reticulated Meissen Strawflower pattern plate (Figs. 188-190), while not as restrained as the double leaf dish of Fig. 177, shows a high degree of workmanship. Nevertheless, absent any proof that it was purchased directly from the manufactory, it has to be classified as decorated outside.

Fig. 188. Plate (Meissen, c. 1770), continuously reticulated, decorated in the Strawflower pattern with later polychrome overdecoration, D 9" (estimated value $250-350).

Fig. 189. Detail of the well of the plate in Fig. 188.

Fig. 190. Mark on the plate in Fig. 188, impressed "6" incised three vertical parallel lines with a horizontal line across them, crossed swords over "XI", possibly a blue painter's mark but cannot be attributed to a particular painter.

Fig. 191. Saucer (Meissen, c. 1740) decorated in the Pagoda and Three Trees pattern, exterior with capuchin brown glaze and decorated with abandon much later by *Pfutscher* during the 19th century, D 5" (*courtesy of Auktionshaus Bergmann, Erlangen, Germany*), (estimated value $500-700).

At the other extreme is truly grotesque overdecoration that comes close to defacing an otherwise valuable object. Such excesses could not have possibly originated in the Meissen Manufactory. An example is afforded by the early cup and saucer shown in Fig. 191, originally in the Pagoda and Three Trees pattern with capuchin brown glaze, and later painted over by a true botcher.

This concludes our survey of Meissen's underglaze blue painting to the end of the Marcolini period. His departure on January 1st, 1814, and death during the same year, marks also the closing of the Blue Painter Room, at least for a while. It took blue painting almost forty years to recover its lost glory and become, in the form of the Blue Onion or *Zwiebelmuster* pattern, the most widely popular and broadly affordable Meissen product from 1860 until today. Numerous new shapes and pattern variants were added to the ever-expanding dinner services to satisfy new customer needs. That story will be told in the next chapter dealing with nineteenth century shapes and patterns.

Chapter II

Blue Onion Renaissance: Mid-nineteenth Century Blue Onion and Related Dinnerware

The Meissen Manufactory During the First Half of the Nineteenth Century

The dawn of the nineteenth century found Meissen at the verge of an economic crisis which only worsened during the first decade. The profound mismanagement of the Manufactory by the Marcolini administration was only part of the problem. War and political unrest in the Ottoman dominated Balkans shut down the Turkish and Russian markets in 1806. Competition from manufactories with more advanced technologies and a lower cost structure compounded the problem. The year 1806 was also the year Prince Elector Friedrich August III of Saxony decided to leave the German Reich and ally himself with Napoleon. In return, Napoleon conferred upon the Prince Elector the title of King. Since then Saxony became a Kingdom.

Choosing the wrong side in the Napoleonic wars dealt severe blows to the Saxon State. On September 1, 1813, Count Marcolini penned his last memorandum to the King. He reported a huge inventory of unsold porcelain worth over 350 thousand Thalers. His recommendation was to stop production immediately! On October 19, 1813, one day after the Battle of Leipzig, the former Prince Elector, now King Friedrich August I, was arrested and brought to Berlin. Saxony was put under the administration of a Russian Governor-General, Prince Repnin. At the end of 1813 Count Marcolini tended his resignation as Director of the Manufactory.

On April 1, 1814, Prince Repnin appointed Carl Wilhelm von Oppel as Director of the Manufactory. Von Oppel, like all of his predecessors, continued to live in Dresden. The day-to-day running of the business was left to Heinrich Gottlieb Kühn, who came in as a hands-on administrator on July 1, 1814. The Russians surrendered control of Saxony soon thereafter and the state was briefly put under the administration of a Prussian Governor-General. In 1815, the King returned from his exile in Berlin. Despite having lost territory and population, Saxony was once again independent. With von Oppel, Kühn, and an ambitious team of young technologists in place, the seeds for the future recovery of the Manufactory were sown. The recovery was further aided by the establishment of a constitutional monarchy in Saxony in 1831, and the establishment of the German Customs Union (*Zollverein*) on January 1, 1834. The latter development was particularly beneficial. By the end of 1834 the Manufactory was once again able to show a profit, the first time it did so since 1790.

Underglaze blue painting did not fare as well. It had been in slow decline throughout the Marcolini Period. In 1776 the Manufactory employed over two hundred painters, twenty-eight of them worked in the Blue Room. That number declined steadily until Kühn dissolved the Blue Room altogether. Its last foreman, Johann Gottlob Möbius, Jr. (we met his father as the blue painter with Mö as his initials), was sent to early retirement. Kühn retained five blue painters to continue producing replacement pieces or filling small orders but strictly on demand. Between 1814 and 1849, the number of blue painters fluctuated between two and five. They were first integrated with the rest of the painting corps (*Buntmaler*), and after 1817 classified together with the green painters (cf. next section) as underglaze painters (*Glasurmaler*). The underglaze painters were once again put under Möbius, Jr. who was called back from retirement to resume his duties as foreman.

During the first half of the nineteenth century Meissen offered a very meager assortment of underglaze blue porcelain. The price list (now called *Preis-Nota*) of 1840 names just a few well-established patterns. These included ordinary blue painting (i.e. Blue Onion), Festoons (cf. Fig. 192), Leafy Edge, and German Flowers.

Fig. 192. Large bowl (Meissen, c. 1830), Festoon pattern, crossed swords mark shown in inset on unglazed bottom, D 15" (*courtesy of Auktionshaus Bergmann, Erlangen, Germany*), (estimated value $400-500).

Technical innovations during the first half of the nineteenth century

The Meissen Manufactory had lost its technological and artistic preeminence after 1760, and during the first half of the nineteenth century its very survival was in question. The manufactories of Berlin, Vienna, and Copenhagen had become serious competitors, with significant technological and artistic contributions of their own. That is after all the reason why examples of their products have been included in this volume. It would be wrong to assume, however, that technical progress in Meissen stood still during this time.

A steady stream of incremental improvements paved the way for rebirth. Four such advances have contributed significantly to expand artistic expression in blue and white (and the related underglaze green) decoration.

The French chemist Jean Hellot had developed the royal blue ground at the Sèvres Manufactory in 1760. Known as *bleu de roí*, it provided a brilliant blue background. White reserves with gilded contours produce a dramatic visual effect when viewed against this background. Since 1766 Meissen tried to reproduce this effect. In December of 1781 the Manufactory invited Carl Friedrich Wenzel, a well-known chemist and high-ranking official of the Freiberg mines to join the Meissen laboratories for a period of time to help develop the technology for royal blue. Wenzel, who had been already consulting with Meissen since 1778 for improving underglaze blue colors, was able to reinvent the royal blue technique in 1782. The technique was also independently invented in the Royal Porcelain Manufactory (KPM) in Berlin around the same time. In this technique the cobalt pigment is applied over the glaze. In a second sharp firing the glaze is brought close to its melting point and the cobalt pigment diffuses into it. In fact, cobalt atoms enter the aluminum-oxygen-silicon network as network modifiers. The artistic effect was obtained at the cost of an additional energy-intensive, and therefore expensive, manufacturing step. Nevertheless, the artists now had one more venue in their quest for blue and white harmony.

Examples of royal blue Meissen are shown in Figs. 4 and 193. The deep round bowl shown in Fig. 4 is also an example of gold-bronze technology. The large shell-shaped bowl of Fig. 193 from the middle of the nineteenth century was decorated with luster gilding, most of it now worn away. Upon close examination one can still see the remnants of elaborate scrollwork.

Fig. 193. Shell-shaped bowl (Meissen, c. 1850), gilded foliate relief on royal blue ground, L 12", W 9.25" (estimated value as is $90-100, with mint gilding $250-300).

Most of the other technical innovations were aimed at cutting manufacturing costs. The English had gotten a competitive advantage by developing inexpensive printing methods on porcelain and pottery. In 1811 Meissen began negotiations with the porcelain and glass enameller Samuel Mohn to acquire his technology of using etched or engraved copper plates for printing on porcelain. The Manufactory bought the technology in 1814 for one hundred Thalers. As Kühn wrote in 1828, the method had been particularly useful in defining the contours of topographical scenes, eliminating the need for complicated drawings prior to painting. In general, however, the Manufactory was not satisfied with the quality of transfer printing and avoided it for nearly a century. Only collectors' plates and commemorative items have been produced using transfer printing. Today such items produced by Meissen are clearly marked with the trade name "Aquatinta." A particularly pleasing example of transfer printing is shown in Fig. 5.

Another way of saving costs would be to expand the palette of underglaze colors, thus eliminating the need for the last firing step(s). A significant advance in this direction was the development in 1817 of an underglaze green color based on chromium oxide. In 1816 Kühn imported fifty pounds of chromite (an ore containing iron and chromium oxides $FeCr_2O_4$) from Vienna, and initiated experiments for the large scale production of chromium(III) oxide, Cr_2O_3. A short time later, sometime during the month of September 1817 the first plates decorated in underglaze green reached the market. This pigment has a much deeper hue than the overglaze green color based on copper oxide. Chromium oxide does not interact chemically with the porcelain body or glaze during sharp firing. That makes the design stand out. The deep green hue of this pigment is particularly conducive to the painting of foliage. This property contributed to its use for foliate patterns like the Vine Leaf pattern (*Grüner Weinblätterkranz* or *Voller grüner Weinkranz* in the catalogs, colloquially *Weinlaubdekor*) developed by Johann Samuel Arnhold. The leaves are applied using a rather complicated stenciling method. The vines and veins of the leaves are free-hand drawings. An admixture of iridium oxide is used to get the black colors (Sterba 1989). The Vine Leaf pattern quickly became popular and competed favorably with Blue

Onion. By the middle of the nineteenth century Meissen catalogs listed 238 different shapes in Blue Onion vs. 261 shapes in the Vine Leaf Pattern. Examples are shown in Figs. 194-198.

Fig. 194. Teapot (Meissen, 1820), Swan-handle shape, in the underglaze chromium green Vine Leaf pattern, H 7.5", W (spout-to-handle) 8" (estimated value $500-600).

Fig. 195. Detail of the vine leaves on the teapot of Fig. 194 highlighted in gold.

Fig. 196. Covered tureen with twisted finial (Meissen, c. 1860), underglaze green Vine Leaf pattern, crossed swords and painter's numeral "61" in underglaze blue, L 10.75", W 6.5", H 6.5" (*courtesy of a private collection*), (estimated value $800-1000).

Fig. 197. A *tête-à-tête* (Meissen, c. 1860) assembled from a harmonious variety of shapes, coffeepot with lid and creamer in the Snake-handle form, sugar bowl with lid in the Swan-handle form, cylindrical cups and saucers derive from earlier Rococo shapes, underglaze green Vine Leaf pattern (estimated value $800-900).

Fig. 198. Coffeepot of assembled *tête-à-tête* shown in Fig. 197 showing details of the shape and pattern, note differences in finials between the Swan- and Snake-handle forms.

Following the success of underglaze green painting, blue and green painters were combined into the new category of underglaze painters (*Glasurmaler*), resurrecting in a sense the defunct Blue Room.

Buoyed by the success of the Vine Leaf Pattern, Meissen tried reissuing some of the older patterns in underglaze green. A curious example (picture not shown) from the von Barsewisch collection is a plate from ca. 1820 decorated in two-tone underglaze green in the Rock and Bird Pattern. It was not a financial success.

Gilding also became the target of cost cutting innovations. As mentioned earlier, in 1827 Kühn developed luster gilding, which is quite durable, uses less gold, does not require a polishing step, and needs a comparatively low firing temperature.

Throughout this period underglaze painting was treated like a stepchild. In 1817 the arcanists developed two other, cheaper formulations for the porcelain body from lower grades of kaolin from Kaschka and Seilitz. The lowest grade material was used exclusively for the manufacture of laboratory equipment and apothecary vessels. Items made out of the second grade material were marked with an underglaze blue Roman numeral II under the crossed swords. Until 1820 all underglaze blue and green decorated ware was manufactured exclusively using this inferior formulation. The approach did not meet with customer acceptance, however, and after 1824 the use of a cheaper porcelain body was discontinued altogether.

The Meissen Manufactory During the Second Half of the Nineteenth Century

Fig. 199. Engraving of the new manufactory complex in the Triebischtal taken from the cover of a 1933 Meissen catalog.

Fig. 200. Main entrance to the Meissen Manufactory today flagged with banners of the crossed swords.

The Meissen Manufactory entered the second half of the nineteenth century in much better shape financially. The vexing economic problems that had threatened the Manufactory's very existence since the beginning of the Marcoloni directorship had been largely overcome. In 1849, in recognition of his many technical achievements, Kühn was promoted to Director of the Meissen Manufactory, a position he retained until his death on January 10, 1870 (Berling, 1911). It is ironic that after having shown his disdain for underglaze blue painting on more than one occasion, it would be Kühn, who would preside over the unparalleled commercial success of the Blue Onion pattern. Advances in manufacturing technology together with the relocation of the Manufactory from the Albrechtsburg to its new facilities in the Triebisch valley increased manufacturing capacity. Active participation in world's fairs drew attention to Meissen's products and also served as inspiration to Meissen's artists and technologists.

As early as 1834 the fuel for kilns had been converted from wood to coal. Mechanical power, however, was still supplied by a rotating drum operated by four large horses. In 1853 this arrangement was replaced by a large steam engine in the basement of the Albrechtsburg. The vibrations from the engine began to cause structural damage to this ancient landmark. The damage was compounded by the soot from the use of coal. Already in 1838 the Saxon Union for the Antiquities (*Sächsischer Altertumsverein*) expressed concern about the deterioration of the historic building. In 1854 the Congress of German Architecture (*Deutsche Architekturversammlung*) demanded that the Manufactory be moved. In 1858 the amount of 300,000 Thalers was voted for a new building to be erected in the Triebisch valley (*Meißen Triebischtal*, the train station one gets off today when visiting the Manufactory). The location would also provide ample water power. The new facilities were built during the years 1860-1864, and the final move took place in 1865. They continue to be the Manufactory's home to this date. Figs. 199-201 show views of the facilities then and now.

Fig. 201. Rear view of the Meissen Manufactory complex today crowned by the crossed swords mark on the rooftop.

The world's fairs also had a great impact on the course of the Manufactory's business and technical developments. Dinner sets in Blue Onion with gilt rim were exhibited at the 1851 World's Fair in London. An expanded service manufactured specifically for the 1862 World's Fair, also in London, was a smashing success. The Blue Onion renaissance had begun! Meissen's annual sales volume for underglaze blue painted porcelain rose from 16,989 Thalers in 1863 to 99,534 Thalers in 1874. In the years between 1881 and 1884 blue painted porcelain comprised over forty percent of all porcelain sold by Meissen.

Following Kühn's death, Moritz Oskar Raithel became director of the Manufactory, a position in which he served with distinction until his retirement in 1895. In 1873 Dr. Julius Ludwig Ferdinand Heintze, a student of the famous German chemist Herman Kolbe, joined the technical staff. Heintze was responsible for many of the late nineteenth century technical developments and he, too, was later rewarded by being named director of the Manufactory.

Technical innovations during the second half of the nineteenth century

In 1875, two years after his arrival in Meissen, Heinze made his first significant contribution to the technology of blue and white porcelain. Over a century and a half had elapsed since Köhler's hesitant first steps into underglaze blue painting. Mass manufacturing was mostly under control, but there were still failures and rejects. Heintze suspected that some of these unpredictable problems may have to do with the composition of the atmosphere inside the kilns. Using the novel techniques of gas analysis he showed that atmospheres that were too oxidizing (rich in oxygen) or sometimes too reducing (excess of carbon monoxide) were detrimental to the process.

Heintze's second great contribution was the reinvention of the *pâte-sur-pâte* technique for the Meissen Manufactory in 1878. The decorating technique known as *pâte-sur-pâte* or paste-on-paste was developed by Gély at the Sèvres Manufactory in France during the 1850s and was used there for striking artistic creations by Marc Louis Solon until Solon's move to the Mintons in England in 1870. The process involves painting in white with slip on an already colored ground prior to glazing. Upon firing, the colored ground shines through the vitrified painting and makes it appear eerily three-dimensional. The slip is made out of clay diluted by a mildly alkaline solution of sodium carbonate. It has a creamy consistency and can be brushed on like any other porcelain pigment. The ground colors must be able to withstand the sharp firing step. The *pâte-sur-pâte* process is often applied on cobalt blue ground and as such it can be viewed as yet another venue for underglaze blue decoration. A particularly attractive and significant example from a private Rochester, New York, collection is given in Fig. 202.

The Sèvres Manufactory exhibited *pâte-sur-pâte* at the 1862 World's Fair in London. Ernst August Leuteritz, Meissen's director of the Modeling Department, upon his return from the Fair recommended that this process was worthy of imitation. The need to develop *pâte-sur-pâte* in Meissen became even more urgent after the 1873 World's Fair in Vienna. After Heintze's successful reinvention of *pâte-sur-pâte*, Meissen quickly closed the gap.

In 1880 the technique of inglaze painting with so called sharp fire colors (*Scharffeuerfarben*) was introduced. In this process an overglaze blue paint made of cobalt alumosilicate powder is used to paint the design over the glaze. During a subsequent sharp firing similar to that used for the manufacturing of royal blue ground the blue colored pigment migrates into the glaze. Unlike the underglaze painting that leads to a sharp white/blue contrast, overglaze painting allows for broad variations in the depth of the blue color. Meissen artists took advantage of this property to generate decorations of breathtaking beauty. A stunning example is the vase shown in Fig. 203 decorated in 1891-1892 and exhibited at the 1893 World's Fair in Chicago. The form was designed by Leuteritz in 1856. The Meissen artist Ernst Moritz Pappermann painted the vase after a frieze by Eduard Bendemann in the Grand Ballroom of the Dresden Palace depicting a gymnastics competition set in ancient Greece. The vase can be seen in the Porcelain Museum at the Meissen Manufactory.

Opposite page:
Fig. 202. Covered urn (Meissen, ca. 1895), form modeled by Michel Victor Acier towards the end of the 18th century, with allegory of Harvest painted in *pâte-sur-pâte* within a grey-pink oval on royal blue ground matching the description of the vase sent to the 1900 World's Fair in Paris, H 12", W 7" (*courtesy of a private collection*), (estimated value $12,000-18,000).

Right:
Fig. 203. Vase (Meissen, 1891-1892) form by Leuteritz in 1856, painted by Ernst Moritz Pappermann after a frieze in the Grand Ballroom of the Dresden Palace by Eduard Bendemann, displayed at the 1893 World's Fair in Chicago (*amateur photograph, reproduced with permission, Meissen GmbH, Meissen, Germany*).

The use of water-based colorants for underglaze blue painting, first developed at the Royal Copenhagen Manufactory, can be traced back to 1888. It involves aqueous solutions of water-soluble salts like cobalt nitrate that can be applied by a brush. Their advantage lies in the fact that they are evenly absorbed into the unglazed porcelain body. A very rigorous drying protocol has to be observed after painting to prevent the color from spreading when the glaze is applied.

Pattern Innovations

The pattern innovations during most of the nineteenth century were largely variations on existing themes, with the Vine Leaf Pattern as the only notable exception. Blue Onion sets with gilt rims are already listed in the 1840 price list. As mentioned earlier, most of the eighteenth century overdecorated Meissen blue and white porcelain received its decoration outside the Meissen Manufactory, probably during the 1830s. Meissen's own overglaze red and gold highlighted Rich Blue Onion pattern was shown to the public during the 1851 World's Fair in London. Though one cannot claim with certainty that the London Fair marks the first introduction of the pattern to the market, this is the earliest archival reference to it. It was still regarded as a "new development" by Meissen's Board of Directors as late as 1852.

The Manufactory was eager to find a replacement to the Blue Onion pattern, even as the pattern was at the height of its commercial success. In 1878 Raithel challenged the Manufactory artists to produce a new underglaze blue pattern. At the same time he asked Carl Ludwig Theodor Graff, director of the Dresden School of the Arts, for a new design contribution. The Manufactory artists came up with a design reminiscent of Japanese motifs and called it the New Fan pattern (*Neues Fächermuster*). The design developed by Graff consisting of complicated arabesques with a central bird sitting on a twig of thorns bears simply his name, *Graffsches Dessin*. Neither of the two patterns could gain any traction in the marketplace.

This situation continued until Ludwig Georg Philipp Sturm, supervisor of painting 1880-1904, began leading blue painting into new directions. He was behind the application of inglaze blue painting with sharp fire colors to monumental pieces like the vase of Fig. 203. Sturm designed the four large porcelain door panels that were installed on the doors of the grand reception room in *Herrenchiemsee*, the palace of Ludwig II, King of Bavaria, in 1886. The actual painting was done by Pappermann and Julius Eduard Braunsdorf.

Around 1883 Sturm designed yet another version of the Blue Onion pattern, borrowing ideas from the Art Nouveau movement. This pattern was known as New Blue Onion (technically it was called "New Stylistically Correct Blue Onion Pattern after Sturm" or *neues stilgerechtes blaues Zwiebelmuster nach Sturm* (!)). Just like the traditional Blue Onion pattern around this time, it was also produced in the overglaze colors red, pink, and green *en camaieu*. Examples of the red version and a "rich," i.e. overdecorated, version from the Doris P. Simonson Collection are shown in Figs. 204 and 205.

Fig. 204. Dinner plate (Meissen c. 1885-1900) New Blue Onion pattern after Sturm, in overglaze purple *camaieu* (courtesy of the Doris P. Simonson Collection).

Fig. 205. Dinner plate (Meissen c. 1885-1900). Rich New Blue Onion pattern after Sturm (courtesy of the Doris P. Simonson Collection).

Fig. 206. Plate (Meissen, c. 1890), Blue Onion Pattern after Dr. Spitzner, a reissue of the three-fruit variant of the Blue Onion pattern (*amateur photograph, reproduced with permission, Meissen GmbH, Meissen, Germany*).

Like the Graff Design and the Fan pattern before it, the New Blue Onion pattern did not attain the popularity its creators had hoped for.

Around 1890 the Manufactory reissued the early eighteenth century "three-fruit" variant of the Blue Onion pattern. It was modeled after an early piece in the collection of Dr. Carl Spitzner, which the Dresden Porcelain Collection purchased in 1890. The pattern was named "Original Blue Onion pattern after Dr. Spitzner" (*Original Zwiebelmuster nach Dr. Spitzner*). The design is remarkably similar to the early eighteenth century examples and could easily fool even experienced collectors. An example of the Dr. Spitzner pattern as laid out on a banquet table in an exhibit by the Meissen Manufactory is shown in Fig. 206, the fully decked table in Fig. 207.

Fig. 207. A table fully decked in the Blue Onion pattern, also exhibiting the plate of Fig. 206 on display in 2001 in the Meissen Manufactory (*amateur photograph, reproduced with permission, Meissen GmbH, Meissen, Germany*).

A Survey of Nineteenth Century Dinner, Dessert, and Breakfast Sets

Up to now we focused our attention on the various underglaze blue (and green) patterns and the blue painters that created them. As we now take up the discussion of traditional breakfast, dinner, and dessert sets and their constituent pieces, our attention will shift to the shapes and their modelers. A service is defined as a set of tableware of uniform color, design, and decoration that are mutually complementary in their use. Dinner services as we conceive of them today were unknown in Europe until the Renaissance. Royalty ate from gold or gold-washed silver utensils, noblemen could afford mostly silver. These utensils, though made of expensive metals, were simple in shape. The rims of plates and vessels for example were plain and round. The concept of a set with unifying decorative elements did not exist.

The first complete Meissen sets were breakfast sets made during the early 1720s. One such set was already described in our discussion of eighteenth century overdecoration (cf. Fig. 149). The shapes continued to be free of any major sculpted elements with the exception of finials and handles of tureens and covered serving pieces until the arrival of Johann Joachim Kaendler in 1731. Kaendler was at the time only twenty-five years old. He was brought in to help Gottlob Kirchner, a modeler since 1727, for the completion of the huge order for the *Japanisches Palais*. During his long tenure at the Manufactory, which ended with his death in 1775, Kaendler created not only the spectacular figurines and gigantic porcelain animal statues for which he is best known, but also numerous dinner services and new shapes for tableware.

When Kaendler first arrived in Meissen, he was appalled by the lack of artistic quality in the modeling department. As he poignantly stated, he found "not one single handle that was done properly" (*keinen rechtschaffenen Henckel*). Between 1732 and 1737 Kaendler created at least four major dinner services for European royalty and very high-ranking noblemen of the Saxon court. These included the set for the Swedish King Adolf Frederik I, the Coronation Set for August III, the set for Count Alexander Joseph von Sulkowski, and most famous of all, in 1737, the Swan Service (*Schwanenservice*) for Count Heinrich von Brühl. The latter set is rumored to have consisted of over 2,000 pieces. Many of these pieces are still in the possession of the von Brühl family, the most spectacular of them are on display in the Dresden Porcelain Collection, and on rare occasions individual pieces are offered at auction. These grand dinner sets were one-of-a-kind, and were made to order. Meissen's first extensive pricelist, printed in 1765, offers only complete breakfast sets to the general public.

Kaendler's greatest impact on Meissen's underglaze blue tableware was his modeling of the New Cutout shape (*Neuer Ausschnitt*). Kaendler created this shape in May of 1745 in response to a request for a service to be decorated with the German Flower Pattern in underglaze blue. The New Cutout with its unmistakable scalloped rim is not an entirely original shape. Chinese ceramic plates with an almost identical rim date back to the Song Dynasty (960-1279). Kaendler correctly recognized that this ancient design would harmonize quite naturally with the Baroque forms of the New Cutout shape. Furthermore this shape is smooth, without any relief decorations, which makes it the ideal canvas for an intricate pattern like the Blue Onion. Since 1820 the New Cutout is the most widely used shape for Blue Onion and related services.

When Kaendler initially modeled the New Cutout shape, he intended it for the middle classes. The sets were rather modest, consisting of a few tens of different pieces. The basic pieces were clearly in the Baroque tradition. By the late nineteenth century the New Cutout had grown to comprise over 500 different pieces. One consequence of this explosive growth was the loss of the purity of its style. As we shall see in the description of the individual pieces, components with neo-classical design elements were gradually introduced into the basic service. Prominent among the modelers who created neo-classical shapes for tableware was Johann Carl Schoenheit who originally modeled the reticulated basket with rams' heads during the second half of the eighteenth century (Fig. 253).

A wide variety of figural elements also play a great role. The finials in the form of a boy or a girl emptying a horn-of-plenty, ubiquitous on tureen and sauceboat covers of the New Cutout, can be traced to the work of another great eighteenth century modeler, Johann Friedrich Eberlein. Grand centerpieces are also included in the Meissen pricelists as items complementary to the basic sets. The inspiration for this nineteenth century "statuary for the table" came from eighteenth century modelers like Carl Christoph Punct. These nineteenth century Rococo Revival centerpieces sought to recapture the splendor of the elaborate dinner parties (*Schauessen*) thrown by the Saxon court during the preceding century, and convey their ambience to the bourgeoisie. Many of the nineteenth century figural centerpieces were creations of Ernst August Leuteritz, Meissen's premier modeler during the nineteenth century, and manager of the modeling department. We will have more to say about these items later. Three other shapes are worth mentioning before we discuss the New Cutout shapes in greater detail. The first, a plainer version of the New Cutout, the so-called "1000-Form", was used for coffee and tea sets and often decorated in the Blue Onion Pattern. Drawings of this form are shown in Sterba's book (Sterba 1989). A cup of this shape is shown in Fig. 208.

The other two shapes are also used for tea and coffee services and are decorated primarily in the Vine Leaf Pattern. The two forms, named after the shape of their handles, are the Swan-Handle shape (*Schwanenhenkel*) and the Snake-Handle shape (*Schlangenhenkel*). The latter was already modeled in 1815 by Johann Daniel Schöne, a couple of years before the development of underglaze green technology that contributed to its popularity. Pieces from both shapes are shown in Figs. 197, 198, and 194. The two shapes are rather similar and over the years they have been mixed and matched to complete sets when pieces were broken. The figure captions provide additional details (for drawings showing the differences between the two shapes cf. Sterba 1989).

Fig. 208. Cup and saucer (Meissen, c. 1860) in the "1000-Form" shape, decorated in the Blue Onion pattern and gilded cup D 2.25", H 2", saucer D 4.5" (estimated value $75-95).

The Basic Dinner Service: Meissen price lists of the eighteenth century (beginning with 1765) do not list complete dinner services, only individual pieces from which customers could assemble sets meeting their needs. During the nineteenth century price lists began to include dinner sets of various sizes and a variety of parts that have changed with time. As an example of the early part of this period, the pricelist of 1840 lists basic dinner services for twelve, eighteen, and twenty-four persons consisting of 80, 124, and 177 pieces respectively. Price lists of the Manufactory from 1840 and 1905 are transcribed below.

List from 1840 for Dinner Services for Twelve, Eighteen, and Twenty-Four Persons Offered By the Royal Saxonian Porcelain Manufactory in Meissen And Its Branch Stores in Dresden and Leipzig

Number of Pieces for Twelve	Number of Pieces for Eighteen	Number of Pieces for Twenty-Four	Description
36	60	72	Dinner Plates, 10.5 inch
12	18	24	Dessert Plates, 9 inch
12	18	24	Soup Bowls, 9.5 inch
1	1	2	Round Tureens
1	1	2	Tureen Underplates
-	-	2	Round Bowls, 16.5 inch
1	2	2	Round Bowls, 14.5 inch
1	2	2	Round Bowls, 13.5 inch
2	-	-	Round Bowls, 11.5 inch
-	-	1	Oval Platter, 21.5 inch
1	2	2	Oval Platter, 20 inch
1	2	-	Oval Platter, 16.25 inch
-	-	2	Oval Platter, 14.25 inch
-	2	4	Salad Bowls, 11.75 inch
2	2	4	Salad Bowls, 10.5 inch
2	2	4	Salad Bowls, 8.5 inch
-	-	4	Comports, 8.25 inch
-	-	4	Comports, 7.5 inch
-	2	4	Comports, 7 inch
-	2	2	Vegetable Tureens, 11.25 inch
2	-	2	Vegetable Tureens, 9 inch
2	4	6	Salt Cellars
1	2	2	Mustard Pots and Ladles
1	2	2	Butter Dishes

The full table lists prices for the sets in a variety of patterns. The most expensive set was decorated overglaze with flowers and 1/4 inch gold borders with a list price of 109 Thaler and 26 Neugroschen for a set for twelve. The price for a complete set for twelve in the plain Blue Onion pattern was 50 Thaler and 5 Neugroschen, and 89 Thaler and 10 Neugroschen for a gilded set. The most expensive blue underglaze set for twelve was decorated with German flowers and gold borders with a list price of 102 Thaler and 8 Neugroschen.

Between 1838 and 1873 the German currency was the Thaler, equal to 30 Neugroschen. One Thaler was equivalent to 0.53 oz. of silver or 0.69 U.S. silver dollars. After 1873 the Reichsmark (RM) and Pfennig system (1 RM = 100 Pfennig) was introduced, with one Thaler equal to three RM.

Note also that in this early table the English system is used with size expressed in inches (*Zoll* in German). The later tables reproduced below use the metric system.

Price List from 1905 for a Dinner Service for Twelve in the Pink Onion Pattern By the Royal Porcelain Manufactory in Meissen (Prices given in Reichsmark and Pfennig)

Number of Pieces	Description	Price (RM) White Border	Price (RM) Gilt Border
12	Soup Bowls, 23.5 cm	48.00	66.00
36	Dinner Plates, 25 cm	144.00	198.00
12	Dessert Plates, 21.5 cm	40.80	52.80
12	Compote Bowls, 16 cm	28.80	40.80
1	Tureen	33.00	42.00
1	Tureen Underplate	24.00	30.00
2	Large Oval Platters, 49 cm	36.00	46.00
2	Small Oval Platters, 36 cm	20.00	28.00
2	Gravy Boats w. Handles	24.00	34.00
1	Sauce Tureen w. Lid	17.00	21.00
3	Gravy Ladles	10.20	13.20
2	Round Bowls, 31 cm	15.00	22.00
2	Covered Vegetables	40.00	52.00
1	Fish Platter, 55 cm	20.00	22.00
2	Square Salad Bowls, 22 cm	22.00	30.00
2	Round Salad Platters, 25 cm	11.00	17.00
2	Square Salad Platters, 20 cm	14.00	18.0
2	Oval Salad Platters, 23 cm	12.00	15.00
1	Mustard Pot and Ladle	7.80	10.90
4	Double Salt Cellars	12.00	16.00

1 inch = 2.54 cm

The same catalog describes a coffee and tea service for twelve consisting of 42 pieces. These include a coffee pot, a teapot, large and small creamers, a sugar bowl, twelve coffee cups (large, as distinct from demitasse or "*Mochatassen*") and saucers, twelve teacups ("*extragross*" i.e. extra large) and saucers, twelve dessert plates, and a cake platter. The price for the set is set to RM 187.00 for plain and RM 253.70 for gilt borders.

The pricelist of 1933 (reproduced in Fig. 209) offers services for six, twelve, and eighteen people consisting of 23, 45-77, and 108 pieces respectively.

Tafelgedecke

Gegenstand	Form Nr.	Maße in cm Inhalt in Liter	Zusammenstellung teilig					
			23	1. Aufst. 45	2. Aufst. 45	60	77	108
Teller, flach	1	25	6	12	12	12	24	36
Teller, flach	3	22	6	12	12	12	12	18
Teller, flach	4	20	–	–	–	–	–	–
Teller, flach	5	17,5	–	–	–	–	–	–
Teller, flach	7	16	–	–	–	12	12	18
Teller, tief	8	24	6	12	12	12	12	18
Terrine, oval f. 12 Personen	16	5	–	1	1	1	1	1
Terrine, oval f. 6 Personen	17	4	1	–	–	–	–	–
Ragoutschüssel	74	33	–	1	1	1	2	2
Ragoutschüssel	75	28	1	–	–	–	–	–
Saucière mit 2 Henkeln	37	26	–	1	2	2	2	2
Saucière mit 2 Henkeln	38	21	1	–	–	–	–	–
Salatnapf, viereckig	84+	23	1	2	2	2	2	2
Salatnapf, viereckig	85+	20	–	1	1	2	–	2
Schüssel, rund, flach	34	35	–	–	–	–	1	2
Schüssel, rund, flach	35	32	–	–	–	–	1	–
Beilageschale, rund	88	25	–	1	–	1	2	2
Beilageschale, oval	92+	25	–	–	–	–	2	–
Bratenschale, oval	64	54	–	–	–	–	–	–
Bratenschale, oval	65	49	–	–	–	1	1	1
Bratenschale, oval	66	42	1	1	1	1	2	2
Bratenschale, oval	67	35	–	–	–	–	1	2
Bratenschale, oval	68	29	–	1	1	1	–	–
Bratenschale, oval	69	25	–	–	–	–	–	–
Bratenschale, oval	70	23	–	–	–	–	–	–
Salz- und Pfeffergefäß	263	10	–	–	–	–	–	–
Salzgefäß	264	5	–	–	–	–	–	–
Senfgefäß	41	16	–	–	–	–	–	–
Senflöffel	44	10	–	–	–	–	–	–
Tafelgedecke, 23teilig			23	–	–	–	–	–
Tafelgedecke, 45teilig, 1. Aufstellung			–	45	–	–	–	–
Tafelgedecke, 45teilig, 2. Aufstellung			–	–	45	–	–	–
Tafelgedecke, 60teilig			–	–	–	60	–	–
Tafelgedecke, 77teilig			–	–	–	–	77	–
Tafelgedecke, 108teilig			–	–	–	–	–	108
Ergänzungsteile:								
Sauce-Terrine m. Untersch.	48	0,8	–	–	–	–	–	–
Buttersaucière	46	0,17	–	–	–	–	–	–
Fischschale	73	55	–	–	–	–	–	–
Grätenschale	61	18	–	–	–	–	–	–
Butterdose	245	21	–	–	–	–	–	–
Messerbänkchen	260	10	–	–	–	–	–	–
Tischkarte	K 271+	10	–	–	–	–	–	–
Fruchtschale	340	30/21	–	–	–	–	–	–
Fruchtschale auf nied. Fuß	342	18	–	–	–	–	–	–
Fruchtschale auf hoh. Fuß	343	23	–	–	–	–	–	–
Konfektschale	361	24	–	–	–	–	–	–
Konfektschale	362	21	–	–	–	–	–	–
Platzteller	947	27	–	–	–	–	–	–

Fig. 209. Reproduction of a section of the 1933 price list of the Meissen Manufactory showing recommendations for dinner services of various sizes.

It is interesting to note that the service for twelve comes in stripped down versions with as few as forty-five pieces or an expanded version consisting of 77 pieces. Nevertheless, none of these sets were truly complete. They had to be augmented with complementary pieces (*Ergänzungsteile*) of which Meissen offered a wide variety. More instructive for future collectors would be the composition of an *actual* nineteenth century dinner service, since it would better reflect the sensibilities of the period. To this end we will discuss a specific Meissen dinner service for twelve in the Blue Onion Pattern and of a known provenance. The service was acquired by a mid-ranking American diplomat in Germany during 1860-1870. This service consisted from the very beginning of the following (118) pieces, all with gilt rims:

12 dinner plates (9 1/2")
12 luncheon plates (9")
12 dessert plates (8")
12 soup bowls (9")
12 small individual salad bowls
12 small individual salt cellars
One large oval covered tureen with figural finial and underplate
One oval covered sauce tureen with figural finial and ladle opening and attached underplate
One open gravy boat with attached underplate
Four covered vegetable dishes with twisted finials
One large salad bowl
Two square salad serving dishes
Five platters of different sizes, ranging from 11" to 20" in length
12 teacups and saucers
12 demitasse and saucers
One waste (slop) bowl
Two low tazzae
Two leaf-shaped dishes
Two round reticulated bowls

Conspicuous by their absence in the above set are teapots, coffeepots, sugar bowls, and cream jugs. In late nineteenth century America sterling silver tea and coffee sets, including magnificent trays, were the norm, particularly in affluent households. Victorian America's preference for fine silver may in part explain the absence of these particular pieces. Similarly, figural centerpieces (which will be discussed in greater length in the next section) are totally absent. This could be entirely due to economic considerations, or perhaps elaborate statues were not part of the dining culture of the United States at that period.

Dessert Services: Meissen began selling complete tea and coffee sets (dessert services) already during the eighteenth century. Meissen's first detailed price list, published in 1765, lists a complete dessert set as consisting of twelve reticulated plates, twelve cups and saucers, six pot-de-crème, one waste bowl, one coffeepot, one cream jug, one teapot, one tea caddy, and other accessories).

Dejeuner sets: Breakfast sets (*dejeuner*) might be for one person (*solitaire*), two people (*tête-à-tête*) or for six. Breakfast sets offered in the pricelist of 1814 consist of an oval tray (plateau), a pair of teacups and saucers, a pair of pot-de-crème, two teaspoons, one coffeepot, one cream jug, one teapot, one sugar bowl, and one tea caddy.

Descriptions of individual shapes

The best way to learn about the many shapes of dinnerware offered by Meissen and other leading porcelain manufacturers and their many imitators is to study their pricelists or catalogs. Meissen catalogs from the second half of the nineteenth century and later are moderately available in antiquarian bookstores specializing in books for collectors. They can also be found in major antiques shows and are frequently offered at auctions including Internet auctions. The shapes described in these older catalogs have survived virtually unchanged to this date and are still in production. Contemporary multilingual catalogs with pictures and precise descriptions of all the shapes available in underglaze blue (as well as all the other patterns) can be obtained from the Meissen Manufactory at modest cost upon request. There is therefore little to be gained from reproducing an entire catalog as part of this book. A representative page from the 1933 pricelist (Fig. 210) is shown in Fig. 211 to convey a feeling for what these prized ephemera look like.

Fig. 210. Cover of the 1933 catalogue of the Meissen Manufactory.

Fig. 211. A page from the 1933 catalogue. Meissen Manufactory catalogues predating WWII, particularly 18th and early 19th century examples, are investment-grade collectible ephemera on their own right.

Instead of publishing pictures of every single piece, we have classified the shapes into broad categories and chose to include only representative examples of each type. We will discuss the various shapes of tableware sequentially as they are used for dinner, dessert, and breakfast (the morning after).

Dinner plates and soup bowls: The 1840 catalog lists two plate sizes, 10 1/2" for dinner and 9" for dessert. By 1933 six different plate sizes were listed without specifying their function, the sizes ranging from 10" to 6.5". That number was expanded once again, so that by 1988 nine different plates with diameters ranging from 10 1/2" to 5 1/2" became available. A 9.5" plate from ca. 1860 with gilt border is shown in Fig. 212 together with smaller plates in Figs. 213-214. Soup bowls range from 7" to 9.5" in diameter. A 9" soup bowl from the same set is shown as part of a place setting in Fig. 215.

Fig. 212. Dinner plate (Meissen, c. 1860), Blue Onion pattern with original gold trim, D 9.5" (estimated value $125-175).

Fig. 213. Bread/butter plate (Meissen, c. 1860), Blue Onion pattern with original gold trim, D 6" (estimated value $100-150).

Fig. 214. Dinner plate (Meissen, c. 1860), Blue Onion pattern with original gold trim, D 9.25" (estimated value $110-160).

Fig. 215. A place setting (Meissen, c. 1860) including soup bowl, dinner plate, small salad bowl, and salt cellar.

Covered soup tureens: Tureens are listed by volume expressed in liters (corresponding approximately to quarts). They can be oval or round and come in three different volumes for each shape. The volume ranges between 1.5 and 4.5 qt. Fig. 216 shows an oval 3 qt. covered tureen with a figural finial. Tureens in the New Cutout shape have foliate scrolled handles curving upward. Oval tureens always come with underplates (sometimes called a *presentoir*) with characteristically upturned handles. These underplates are often mistaken as fish platters.

Fig. 216. Covered tureen and underplate (*presentoir*) (Meissen, c. 1860) figural finial with girl holding the mouth of the horn-of-plenty with her left hand, Blue Onion pattern with original gold trim, tureen L 12", W 8", underplate L 17", W 11", total H 11" (estimated value $2,500-3,000).

The tureen covers have either a twisted or a figural finial. An example with a twisted finial is seen in Fig. 217.

Fig. 217. Covered tureen with twisted finial (Meissen, c. 1860), Blue Onion pattern with original gold trim (courtesy of the Doris P. Simonson Collection).

The figural finials of a boy and a girl clad in tunics holding on to a horn-of-plenty derive from eighteenth century models by Eberlein. We have already encountered them in the matched pair of tureens with boy and girl finials in Figs. 125-127. In those examples the figures look at each other, the girl gazing to the left the boy to his right towards her. Figs. 218 and 219 show details of the figural finial for a ca. 1860 tureen in the Blue Onion pattern with gilt rim. The figure is that of a girl based on her hair tied back in a bun. She is gazing to the left and emptying flowers from a horn-of-plenty whose mouth she holds with her left hand.

Fig. 218. Detail of the little girl on the tureen of Fig. 216, frontal view.

Fig. 219. Detail of the little girl on the tureen of Fig. 216, side view showing her hair tied back in a bun.

Covered sauce tureens and sauceboats: Covered sauce tureens were modeled with an attached underplate and came in two sizes as measured by volume. They were either oval or round. Figs. 220 and 221 show a 1/4 qt. tureen with a twisted finial from ca. 1860 and a 1/2 qt. tureen with a figural finial from the same set as the larger tureen already described. The figural finial in this case is that of a boy, also gazing to the left and holding the mouth of the horn-of-plenty with his right hand. The two figures can be made to look at each other when the tureens are arranged face to face. Contemporary sauce tureens are larger and taller. Sauceboats like the one shown in Fig. 222 are a mid-nineteenth century augmentation of the original New Cutout form, although their basic form goes as far back as 1735 (Miedtank, 2001).

Fig. 220. Covered sauce tureen with attached underplate (Meissen, c. 1860), twisted finial, Blue Onion pattern, bowl L 5.75", W 3.25", underplate L 9", W 5.25" (estimated value $300-400).

Fig. 221. Covered sauce tureen with attached underplate (Meissen, c. 1860), figural finial with boy holding the mouth of the horn-of-plenty with his right hand, Blue Onion pattern with original gold trim, tureen L 6.75", W 5.25", underplate L 10.5", W 7" (estimated value $1,000-1,500).

Fig. 222. Open gravy boat (Meissen, c. 1860) with circular handles and attached underplate, Blue Onion pattern with original gold trim, gravy boat L 8.5", W 6.5", underplate L 10.5", W 6.25" (estimated value $400-500).

Vegetable tureens and dishes: Vegetables were served in covered rectangular vegetable dishes or round vegetable tureens. The covers of the rectangular dishes had exclusively twisted finials, the round tureens had either twisted or figural finials. The sizes of the rectangular dishes varied from 8" to 15" in the long dimension. An example 11" by 8 1/4" is shown in Fig. 223.

Fig. 223. Covered vegetable dish (Meissen, c. 1860), rectangular with twisted finial, Blue Onion pattern with original gold trim, L 11", W 8.25" (estimated value $500-600).

A round vegetable tureen, 9" in interior diameter, part of a set without gilding is shown in Figs. 224-226, together with details of its figural finial. The handles of the vegetable tureens are foliate but flat, distinguishing them from those of the soup tureens. The figure is that of a boy and he again uses his right hand to hold the mouth of the horn-of-plenty.

Fig. 224. Covered vegetable tureen (Meissen, c. 1860), figural finial with boy holding the mouth of the horn-of-plenty with his right hand, Blue Onion pattern, L 13", H 8.5" (estimated value $850-1,000).

Fig. 225. Detailed side view of tureen finial in Fig. 224.

Fig. 226. Detailed rear view of tureen finial in Fig. 224.

Salad serving pieces and relish dishes: The salad in Europe is eaten like a side dish i.e. *together* with the main course not *before* as might be the case with *hors d'oeuvre*. It would have been brought to the table in a deep square salad bowl like the one in Fig. 227. The bowl was decorated both on its interior and exterior surface. The price list of 1840 lists three sizes (11 3/4", 10 1/2", and 8 1/2"), later in the century, the largest available size had an edge length of 10" like the one shown in the figure. Shallow square open containers are also listed as salad serving dishes and may have also been used for other side dishes that were served cold. Four sizes are listed with edge lengths varying from 10 1/2" to 6 3/4", the one shown in Fig. 228 having a length of 9".

Fig. 227. Deep salad bowl (Meissen, c. 1860), Blue Onion pattern with original gold trim, L 10" (estimated value $600-800).

Fig. 228. Square salad serving dish (Meissen, c. 1860). Blue Onion pattern with original gold trim, L 9" (estimated value $300-400).

Another shape that is sometimes mistaken as a pudding or cake mold, because of its fluted sides, actually is also a salad bowl. An example is shown in Fig. 229.

Fig. 229. Salad bowl (Meissen, c. 1860), round with fluted sides, Blue Onion pattern with original gold trim, D 10" (*courtesy of the Doris P. Simonson Collection*).

An individual small salad bowl would have been part of a place setting, as shown in Fig. 215. A large assortment of relish dishes with two, three, and four compartments is also typical; examples are shown in Figs. 230 and 231.

Fig. 230. Divided relish dish (Meissen, c. 1860), two shell-shaped compartments with central vertical handle, Blue Onion pattern, W 11" (*courtesy of Auktionshaus Bergmann, Erlangen, Germany*), (estimated value $40-450).

Fig. 231. Divided relish dish (Meissen, c. 1860), three shell-shaped compartments with central vertical handle, Blue Onion pattern with original gold trim, W 13.25" (*courtesy of the Doris P. Simonson Collection*).

Platters: In Continental European ceramics, platters come in two basic shapes, oval meat platters for serving roasts and somewhat more elongated fish platters. Today, Meissen offers meat platters in eight different sizes. The dining service from ca.1860 considered here entailed five different sizes of meat platters. The fish platter is more elongated, typically 21 1/4" by 10". Pictures of a meat and a fish platter are shown in Figs. 232 and 233 respectively. The elongated form of a fish platter necessitates a modification of the basic Blue Onion Pattern. Instead of the four pairs of fruits around the edge, six pairs are needed to complete the design.

Fig. 232. Oval meat platter (Meissen, c. 1860), Blue Onion with original gold trim, L 15.75", W 11.25" (estimated value $500-800).

Fig. 233. Fish platter (Meissen, c. 1860), Blue Onion with original gold trim, L 21.25", W 10" (estimated value $800-900).

Salts: Salt was an expensive and prized commodity during the Middle Ages and early Renaissance and was presented in a grand and ornate container, the master salt cellar. Salt gradually lost its significance and the ostentatious salt cellars were replaced by the glorious centerpieces we will consider below. Nevertheless, elaborate figural master salts are still listed in the pricelists from c. 1905. The 1903 and later price lists describe the same objects as figures holding bowls and list them together with other statuary for the table. We have followed the latter convention to keep the discussion of all figural pieces together.

There is some confusion about certain shell-shaped dishes. They are classified as either salts or dishes for serving ice cream. Here they are considered as ice cream dishes (consistent with their classification in older catalogues) and described together with shapes for the dessert table. A shape classified unambiguously as a salt cellar is the small leaf-shapes dish with handle from ca. 1860, shown in Figs. 234 and 235. It is about 4" by 3" and represents the middle size of three still offered today. This is a very old shape, a direct descendant of underglaze blue, as well as polychrome Chinese antecedents, that was already produced in Böttger red stoneware and gilded by Irminger around 1710. It is decorated with relief foliage on the underside.

Fig. 234. Salt cellar (Meissen c. 1860), Blue Onion with original gold trim, L 4", W 4" (estimated value $125-175).

Fig. 235. Underside of the salt cellar shown in Fig. 234 showing the foliate relief decoration.

Small, two-compartment vessels with upright handles are also classified as salt cellars. The details of an example in the Japanese Table Pattern or (*Tischchenmuster*) are shown in Figs. 334 and 335. This pattern is discussed separately, together with other overdecoration, in a subsequent section. A small dish, shown in Fig. 215 as part of a place setting, was presumably intended as a salt cellar.

Cutlery, knife rests, and napkin rings: The burgeoning number of Blue Onion accessories towards the end of the nineteenth century included such things as a variety of handles for all sorts of specialized forks and knives, knife rests, and napkin rings. Examples of cutlery with porcelain handles in the Blue Onion pattern are shown in Figs. 236 and 237. The metal part of the cutlery might have been forged locally within the city of Meissen as indicated in one of the pictures, or in one of the many prominent German metal ware factories. The knife rests were generally very plain; an unusual one dating probably somewhat later than the time period within the scope of this book is shown in Fig. 238. It has a naturalistic feel to it resembling a twig and falls possibly into the Art Nouveau period. The napkin ring in Fig. 239 was actually manufactured by the factory of Brothers Schoenau in Hüttensteinach during the first quarter of the twentieth century.

Fig. 236. Cutlery (Meissen, c.1860), three matching pairs of knives and forks, Blue Onion with crossed swords mark at the base of the handle shown in the insert, metal part by Lehmann of Meissen, L 8.25"/9.5" (*courtesy of Auktionshaus Bergmann, Erlangen, Germany*), (estimated value $400-500).

Fig. 237. Cutlery (Meissen c. 1860), two pairs of knives and forks, Blue Onion pattern (*courtesy of the Doris P. Simonson Collection*).

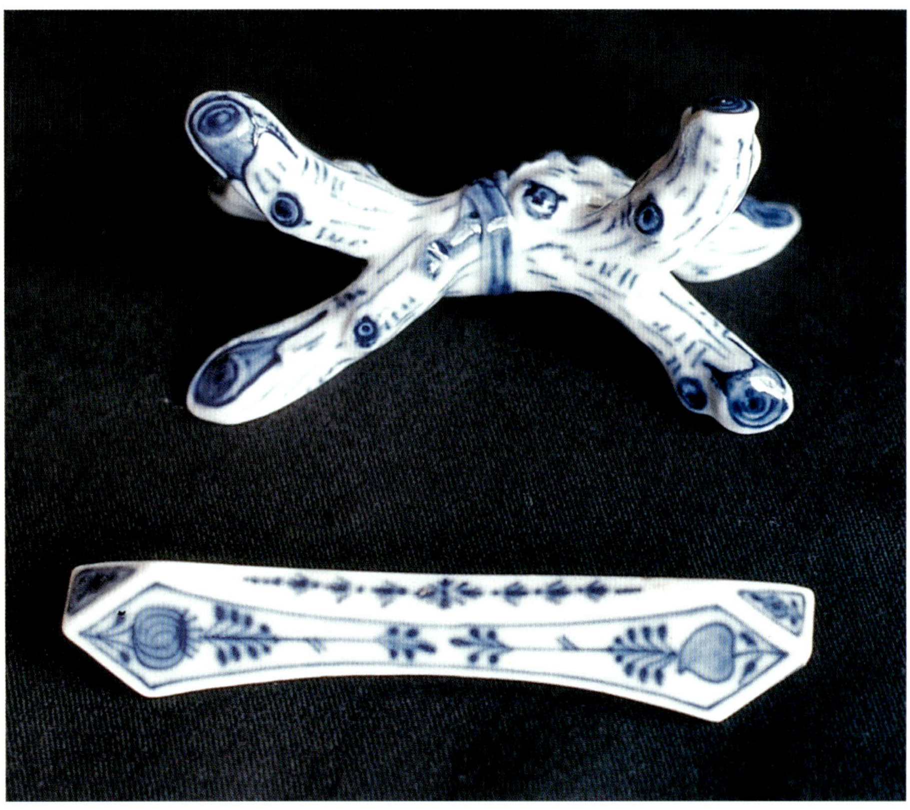

Fig. 238. Two knife rests (Meissen c. 1860 and 20th century), both in the Blue Onion pattern, the lower is of classical shape, the upper (rarer) example is from c. 1900 with an intricate Art Nouveau shape (*courtesy of the Doris P. Simonson Collection*).

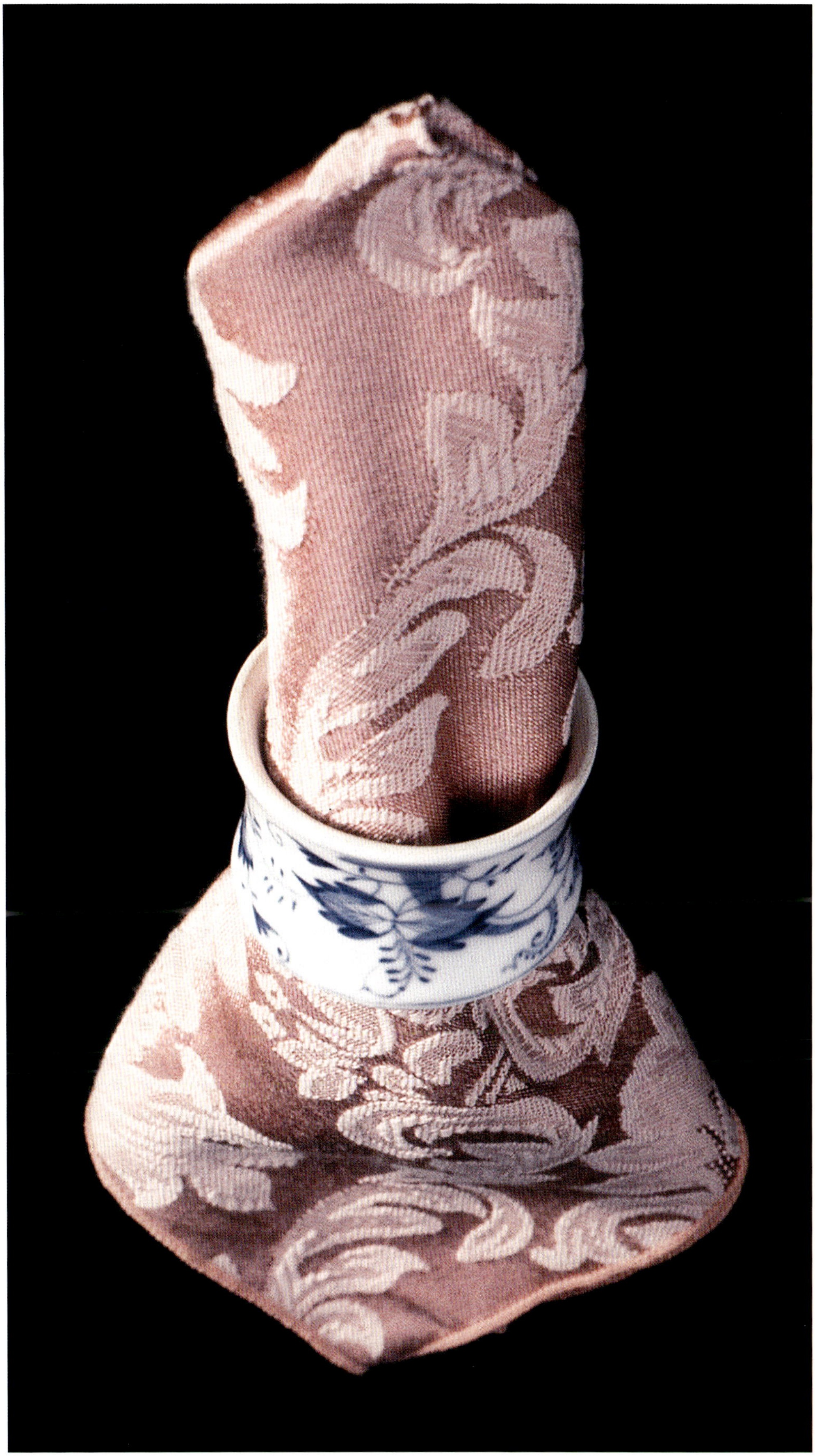

Fig. 239. Napkin ring (Brüder Schoenau Hüttensteinach, c. 1902-30), relatively recent imitation of the Blue Onion pattern by a Thuringian manufactory imitating Meissen shapes and patterns, mark on the inside surface of the ring consists of intersecting, slightly curved underglaze blue lines feigning a crossed swords mark with capital letters "H" above and below (estimated value $15-35).

Other dinner table accessories not shown here include mustard pots, butter dishes and cheese domes, cruets for oil and vinegar, trivets, breadboards, and ladels. More recent items like meat tenderizers, mortars and pestles, rolling pins, hour glasses, strainers, funnels, clock faces, and many others are part of an expanded "kitchen utensils" strategy (*Küchengeräteprogramm*) that was launched in 1989 (Miedtank 2001).

Porcelain for the dessert table: Sweetmeats are the desserts that made up the final or sweet (as opposed to savory) course of a sumptuous dinner. Typical sweetmeats included dried, candied or spiced fruits, creams, custards, jellies and marmalades, various baked goods and assorted confectionery as well as fresh fruits. It is clear from this list that there were two types of sweetmeats, dry and wet. Sweetmeats were originally served in gilt silver containers, but during the sixteenth century glass and Chinese porcelain were preferred because of their neutral taste. The dessert was after all the culmination of a festive dinner and the most impressive and expensive pieces of the service were used to present it. Fine Venetian glass with delicate enamel decoration was used for the frothy, creamy or syrupy (wet) sweetmeats. Plates and serving pieces for dry sweetmeats were shaped with a decorative reticulated edge. The reticulation (even to this day) is hand-pierced and is a value-adding step that makes the item more distinguished and expensive. The kind of reticulation typically encountered in eighteenth century plates is a basket weave reticulation that runs continuously around the edge without interruption. Examples from this period were already shown. Plates with this type of reticulation are still mentioned in the pricelists from 1905 as fully reticulated (*ganz durchbrochen*). Full reticulation is prone to damage. The classic dessert plates of the nineteenth century have a modified type of reticulation, and are listed as reticulated with cartouches (*durchbrochen mit Schildern*). The floral decoration on the cartouches is borrowed from the Strawflower Pattern. A third kind of more elaborate reticulation is the rosette reticulation (*Rosetten-Durchbruch*).

Reticulated plates and bowls: The typical dessert plate is 8" in diameter though later price lists include 6" and 9 1/2" dessert plates. They were issued as reticulated with cartouches as well as with the rosette reticulation. A reticulated 8" dessert plate together with a detailed view of the pattern is shown in Figs. 240 and 241.

Fig. 240. Reticulated dessert plate (Meissen, c. 1860), plate well decorated in the Blue Onion pattern, the border reticulation is interrupted with three cartouches decorated with motifs borrowed from the Indian Flower pattern, D 8" (estimated value $100-150).

Fig. 241. Detailed view of the well of the plate shown in Fig. 240.

Reticulated bowls commonly have five cartouches as opposed to the plates which have only three. Bowls with three cartouches are also known, but they are quite infrequent and not pictured in recent catalogs. Figs. 242, 243, and 244 show bowls with three and five cartouches respectively.

Fig. 242. Reticulated bowl (Meissen, c. 1860). Blue Onion pattern with three cartouches with Indian Flower decoration, D 9.5" (estimated value $400-450).

Fig. 243. Reticulated bowl (Meissen, c. 1860), Blue Onion pattern with original gold trim and five cartouches with Indian Flower decoration, D 9" (estimated value $500-550).

Fig. 244. Another view of the bowl in Fig. 243 showing decoration of the bowl interior.

Examples of the more sophisticated and labor-intensive rosette reticulation are afforded by the gilded bowl and serving plate from ca. 1860 shown in Figs. 245 and 246.

Fig. 245. Rosette-reticulated bowl (Meissen, c.1860), border with rosette-reticulation outlined in underglaze blue, well in the Blue Onion pattern with original gold trim, D 9" (estimated value $600-650).

Fig. 246. Rosette-reticulated serving plate (Meissen, c. 1860), border with rosette-reticulation outlined in underglaze blue, well in the Blue Onion pattern with original gold trim, D 9" (estimated value $400-450).

Waste bowls (known as slop bowls) for the disposal of waste such as tea leaves, coffee grinds, shells, bones, etc. would also be part of the table, and one is shown in Fig. 247 with its underplate.

Fig. 247. Slop bowl with undertray (Meissen, c. 1860), part of a table set for the dessert in the Blue Onion pattern with original gold trim, D 6", H 2.5" (estimated value without underplate $200-300).

Tazzae, comports, and cake plates: Footed containers for both dry and wet sweetmeats have always added to the elegance of a well-dressed dessert table. A tazza is a wide shallow bowl set on a stem. Tazzae may be plain or reticulated depending on their intended use. The stems can be quite diverse as seen in Figs. 248 and 249. The shortest of the tazzae (Fig. 249) has a trumpet-shaped base. The taller stems in later pieces have a knob-like detail about halfway up the stem. Rarer, and possibly restricted to the middle of the nineteenth century, is the tazza of intermediate height (the shorter of the two in Fig. 248) lacking the detail on the stem.

Fig. 248. Two tazzae (Meissen, c. 1860) of different heights and different stem designs (see text for details). Blue Onion pattern with original gold trim, D 8.75", H 4.5", and 5", the taller stem having a knob (estimated value $450-550).

Fig. 249. Reticulated tazza (Meissen, c.1860) on a trumpet base Blue Onion pattern with original gold trim, H 3", D 8" (estimated value $400-500).

Comports (compote is a misnomer recently gaining acceptance) are deeper bowls similar to the reticulated bowls of Figs. 242 and 243 set on stems similar to those of tazzae. In addition, containers supported on dolphin feet like the one shown in Fig. 250 are also classified as comports in some early Meissen catalogues. An overdecorated comport without reticulation is shown in Fig. 337.

Fig. 250. Rosette-reticulated comport (Meissen, c. 1860) supported on dolphin feet, Blue Onion pattern, D 10" (courtesy of the *Doris P. Simonson Collection*).

Cake plates are similar to tazzae but almost completely flat, with diameters ranging from 12 1/2" to 14 1/2". They are supported by short stems and unlike tazzae or comports, they are not decorated on their underside, since it is not exposed to viewing.

Baskets: Reticulated baskets were intended for rolls, sweetbreads or possibly fruit. Their shapes ranged from the modest breadbasket of Fig. 251 to the intricate and elaborate shapes of Figs. 252 and 253. All were offered in a variety of sizes varying from 10" to 20". The basket shown in Fig. 252 was originally modeled by Kaendler.

Fig. 251. Reticulated basket (Meissen, c. 1860), with twisted handles, Blue Onion pattern with reticulation interrupted by four cartouches decorated Indian Flowers and original gold trim, 10" (*courtesy of a private collection*).

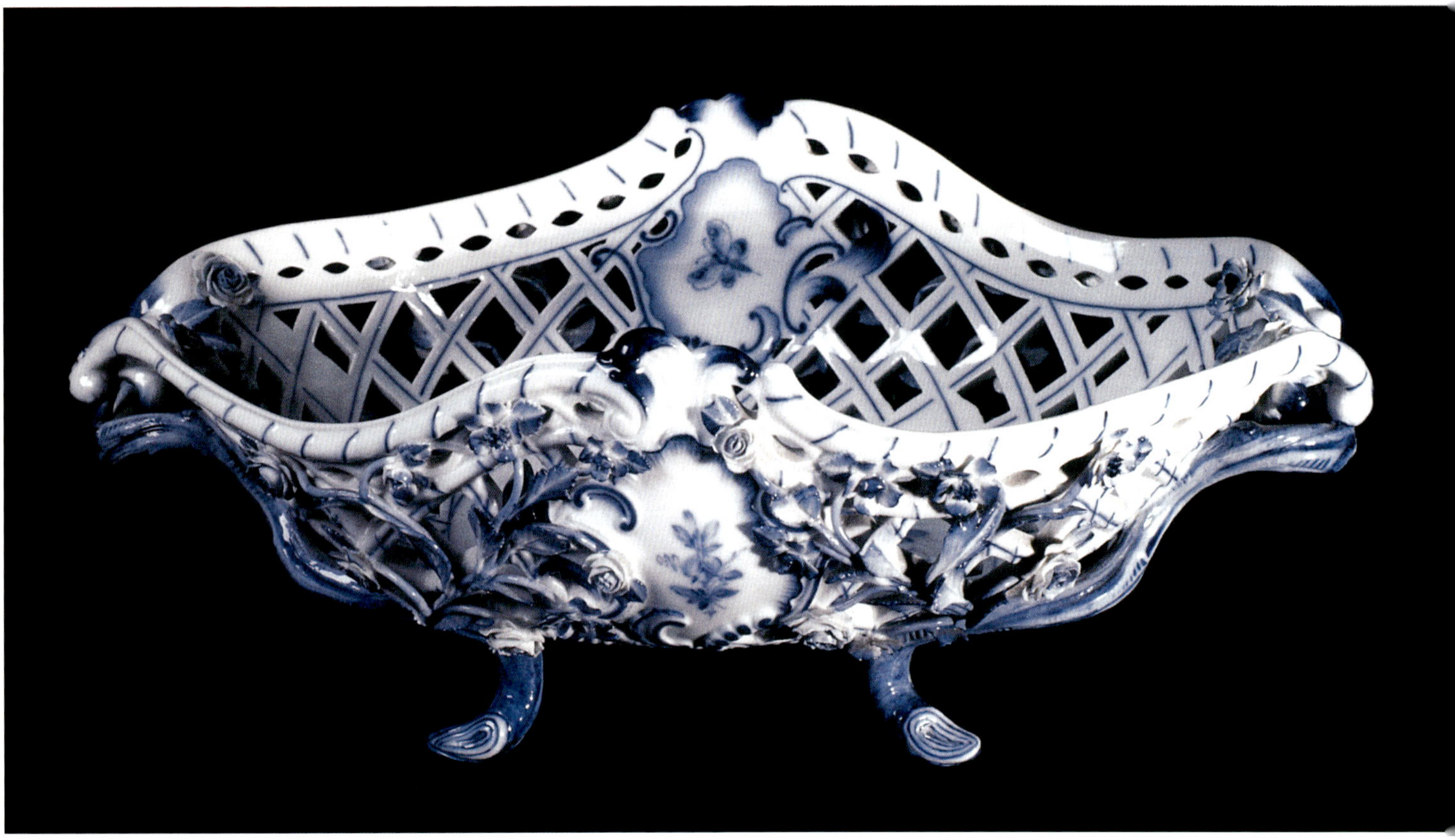

Fig. 252. Reticulated basket (Meissen, c. 1860), encrusted with applied flowers and foliage emerging from slender stems that form the handles and end as four feet supporting the basket, reticulation interrupted by cartouches painted with insects and sprigs of flowers, interior decorated with bouquets of German Flowers, all in underglaze blue, L 15", W 8", H 6" (estimated value $800-1,100).

Fig. 253. Figural basket (Meissen, c. 1860) with ram's heads, applied festoons, and terminating in four ram's feet, unusual reticulation pattern outlined in underglaze blue, cartouches with Indian Flowers, interior in the Blue Onion pattern, L 15" (courtesy of *Auktionshaus Bergmann, Erlangen, Germany*), (estimated value $2,400-2,800).

The most elegant baskets are those supported by figural groupings. These and other vessels with figural parts are described in a separate section. Another popular shape for the serving of condiments or dry sweetmeats is the leaf-shaped dish. The original elegant form (Fig. 89) with applied flowers at the base of the handles typical of the eighteenth century gave way to the shape shown in Fig. 254. In this shape the handle is a simple twig or stump without further decoration.

Punchbowls: These were offered in 3, 4, 5, and 6 qt sizes with or without handles. A quintessential characteristic of the punchbowl shape is the finial in the form of a sliced citrus fruit. An example of the 5 qt. size without handles is shown in Fig. 255.

Fig. 254. Leaf-shaped dish (Meissen, c. 1860) in the Blue Onion pattern with original gold trim, L 9", W 7" (estimated value $275-325).

Fig. 255. Punch bowl (Meissen, c. 1860) with sliced citrus fruit finial, 5 qt. size, Blue Onion pattern (*courtesy of a private collection*).

Coffee, tea, and chocolate pots: In the early catalogs these were often listed by their capacity in serving cups rather than their volume in metric units. Coffeepot size ranged from one to twelve cups. Coffeepots with a capacity for three or six cups must have been the most popular sizes as they are commonly encountered in the antiques market. Teapot sizes ranged from one to ten cups, chocolate pot size from two cups to twelve.

Sugar bowls: These could be round, as in the original New Cutout service, or in quatrefoil form. In the early catalogs sugar bowls were offered in three different sizes and again the middle size appears to have been the most common. Fig. 256 shows a round sugar bowl, 4" in diameter, with no gilding. The quatrefoil shaped sugar bowl shown with the breakfast sets is also mid-size (4" by 3.25"). Both shapes have lids with rose bud finials, a characteristic of the New Cutout service but also of derivative forms.

Cream Jugs: Rich thick cream has always been part of the enjoyment of a good cup of coffee in Central Europe. The jugs came in seven different sizes and two basic shapes, either with or without feet. Both shapes are shown with the dejeuner sets of Figs. 269 and 268.

Caddies: Tea caddies changed very little through the centuries. Chinese export, Meissen, other continental and British caddies all have the same basic shape. Meissen caddies were offered in two sizes. Fig. 257 shows the smaller one (2.75" tall) from the nineteenth century in the Blue Onion pattern with missing lid. The larger (3.5" tall) caddy from the eighteenth century with the quaint Frolicking Putti from the von Barsewisch Collection is shown in Fig. 147.

Fig. 256. Sugar bowl (Meissen, c. 1860), Blue Onion pattern, H 4.75", D 4" (estimated value $175-225).

Fig. 257. Tea caddy with missing lid (Meissen, c. 1860), Blue Onion pattern, H 2.75", L 2.25", W 1.5" (estimated value as is $90-100, with lid $175-250).

Cups and saucers, demitasse and pots-de crème: The original cups and saucers for the New Cutout service have the characteristic scalloped rim with curves and points and handles shaped as intertwined branches terminating in leaves. They came as teacups and in a smaller size as demitasse for mocha (Fig. 258). Later a teacup of a different shape was added to the New Cutout service specifically for the breakfast table (shown in the discussion of dejeuner services).

Fig. 258. Mocha cup and saucer (Meissen, c. 1860), Blue Onion pattern with original gold trim, cup H 1.88", D 2.5", saucer D 4.13" (estimated value $150-175).

The Blue Onion pattern (and other underglaze blue patterns) was also produced on quatrefoil forms like the sugar bowl and the teacup and saucer of Figs. 259 and 260. The quatrefoil cups and saucers have smooth rims and their relation to the traditional New Cutout service is unclear. The price list of 1933 for the New Cutout service offers a choice of cups with scalloped (*geschweift*) or smooth (*glatt*) rims.

Fig. 259. Quatrefoil cup and saucer (Meissen, c. 1860), Blue Onion pattern, cup 3.25" by 3", saucer 5" by 4.38", total height 2.5" (estimated value $100-125).

Fig. 260. Decorated interior of the cup shown in Fig. 259.

Interesting in this respect are a diminutive demitasse and saucer with gilt rim in the Rock and Bird pattern shown earlier in detail in Figs. 102-104. In fact the cup and saucer are small enough to have been parts of a toy set.

Hot chocolate, chaudeaus (*Weinschaumsaucen*), and sorbets might have been enjoyed from covered cups like the lidded pots de crème shown in Figs. 261 and 262 or the covered cup and saucer of Fig. 263.

Fig. 261. A pair of pot-de-crème (Meissen, c. 1860) lids with rose bud finials, H 3.5" (estimated value $375-450 the pair).

Fig. 262. Another view of the pot-de-crème of Fig. 261.

Fig. 263. Covered cup and saucer (Meissen, c. 1860), Blue Onion pattern with original gold trim, cup D 4", saucer D 6.5", H 5" tall (*courtesy of the Doris P. Simonson Collection*).

Ice cream would have been served on shallow dishes like the ones described in Figs. 264 and 265. As customs evolved and ice cream containers changed, these shapes began being listed as salt cellars.

Eggcups and associated breakfast items: Meissen egg cups did not change much through the end of the nineteenth century. During the twentieth century many different and unique shapes were invented and they have become highly desirable collectibles. Our discussions centers on classical pieces that come in basically three shapes, with or without an attached underplate, or with a domed pedestal. An eighteenth century eggcup without underplate with Indian Flower decoration from the Marcolini period was shown in Fig. 55. A nineteenth century eggcup with the typical scalloped (and in this case gilt) rim of the New Cutout shape and decorated in the Blue Onion pattern is shown in Fig. 266. In this case the underplate is attached to the eggcup.

During the second half of the nineteenth century egg cups might have been brought to the table using a special and rarely encountered étagère on royal blue ground, capable of holding six eggcups and a master salt (Fig. 267).

Fig. 264. Ice cream dish (Meissen, c. 1860), sometimes also considered as a salt cellar, shell-shaped with scrolled handle, Blue Onion pattern, L 4.5", W 3.75", H 1.5" (estimated value $175-200).

Fig. 265. Ice cream dish (Meissen, c. 1860), sometimes also considered as a salt cellar, shell-shaped with foliate handle, Blue Onion pattern, L 5", W 4.25", H 1" (estimated value $100-125).

Fig. 266. Egg cup with attached underplate (Meissen, c. 1860), Blue Onion pattern with original gold trim, H 3", underplate D 4.5" (estimated value $125-150).

Fig. 267. Egg cup étagère with egg cups and master salt. (Meissen, c. 1860). Decorated in royal blue and gold bronze with a relief foliate ornamentation and handle shaped as intertwined twigs (estimated value $1000-1250), H 11.75" (*courtesy of Auktionshaus Bergmann, Erlangen, Germany*).

Later egg pans became more common. Again they are found in essentially two shapes, resting either on a flat bottom or on three volute feet as shown in Fig. 331.

Dejeuner Sets; The solitaire and the tête-à-tête: Some of the same pieces used for the dessert table could be arranged on a tray to enjoy one's morning coffee, either in solitude as the name *solitaire* implies, or in an intimate twosome or *tête-à-tête*. Figs. 268 and 269 show assemblies of the basic pieces laid out for the two configurations. Note the two different sizes for the coffeepots and cream jugs. The sets are shown as assembled out of the original New Cutout shapes. Later special teacups and teapots specifically for breakfast use were added to the assortment. A dejeuner teacup is shown in Fig. 270. A typical tray for serving breakfast or afternoon tea for two is shown in Fig. 271.

Fig. 268. Breakfast *solitaire* service (Meissen, c. 1860). The service is similar to a *tête-à-tête*, but with a smaller coffeepot, H 6.25", W 5" spout to handle, capacity 2 cups, and a smaller footed cream jug H 3", W 3.25" spout to handle, 0.075 qt. capacity, all pieces with original gold trim (estimated value for complete set $1,000-1,400).

Fig. 269. Breakfast *tête-à-tête* service (Meissen, c.1860). The service consists of a tray (17.5" by 12.5"), a large coffeepot H 8", W 6" spout to handle, capacity 6 cups, a large cream jug with round foot rim H 5", W 4.5" spout to handle, 0.5 qt. capacity, a quatrefoil sugar bowl L 3.25", W 4" and two cups and saucers, all pieces with original gold trim (estimated value of set 1,300-1,750).

Fig. 270. Dejeuner cup and saucer (Meissen, c. 1860), Blue Onion with original gold trim, interior of cup decorated with small Indian Flower, cup H 2", D 3.75", saucer D 5.5" (estimated value $160-180).

Fig. 271. Tray (Meissen, c.1860) for serving one or two people breakfast or afternoon tea, Blue Onion pattern with original gilding, L 17.5", W 12.5" (estimated value $400-500).

Statuary for the Table: Meissen and many of the other major nineteenth century manufacturers of porcelain tableware included impressive figural pieces in their dinner services. These figures were the scaled-down cultural descendents of the sugar and tragacanth paste sculptures of the royal confectioners of the seventeenth and early eighteenth centuries, and the later, monumental porcelain centerpieces on display at the *Schauessen* of the nobility. Beginning with the middle of the nineteenth century, it was the turn of the bourgeoisie to enjoy the visual splendor of this "statuary for the table" as it has been called by some authors.

Figural tableware pieces of the nineteenth century by Meissen are as crisp and carefully modeled as the Manufactory's famous figurines. After all, they trace their origins to the work of the master modelers of the eighteenth century like Punct, Eberlein, and even Kaendler himself. They owe their resurgence to Leuteritz, Meissen's renowned master modeler of the nineteenth century. Unfortunately, while Meissen figurines maintain their technical and aesthetic excellence to our day, figures on tableware show a marked decline in their crispness of detail after about 1890.

Figural shapes include salts, sweetmeat dishes, multi-tiered sweetmeat trays (étagères), centerpieces, and candelabra. Here they will be classified as objects with a single figure, pairs of figures, or figural groupings.

Most objects with a single figure are actually pairs of objects complementing each other with a male and a female figure. A typical example is the pair of salts consisting of two baskets straddled by a male and female figure. Such a pair is shown in Fig. 272 holding flowers, the male with his right hand, the female with her left, reflecting the traditional convention already encountered on tureen finials. The pair of sweetmeat dishes with reclining male and female figures is Meissen's best known and most widely copied and forged example of figural tableware. They are typically encountered in two sizes. Figures 273-275 show views of the larger size, which is rarely found with gold highlights and flower encrustations on the bowl.

Fig. 272. Pair of figural salts (Meissen, c. 1860), matching pair of male and female figures gazing at each other. H 5", L 5.5", W 2.5" (estimated value $1,100-1,600 for the pair).

Fig. 273. Figural sweetmeat dish (Meissen, c. 1860), reclining male presenting a sweetmeat dish with gold highlights and rare applied flowers, L 13" (*courtesy of the Doris P. Simonson Collection*).

Fig. 274. Another view of the sweetmeat dish of Fig. 273.

Fig. 275. Figural sweetmeat dish (Meissen, c. 1860), reclining female presenting a sweetmeat dish with gold highlights and rare applied flowers, companion piece of dish in Fig. 273, L 13" (*courtesy of the Doris P. Simonson Collection*).

Etageres are two or three tiered serving trays for the presentation of dry sweetmeats culminating in a male or female figurine. They are made of progressively smaller (nesting) reticulated plates decorated also on their underside, which is after all in plain view. This is how authentic etageres can be differentiated from fantasy pieces made from dessert plates. Note also that there is no such thing as a single tier étagère with a figural top. A pair of two-tier etageres in the Blue Onion pattern with the figurines of a younger man and a younger woman on top is shown in Figs. 276-279 together with details of the figurines. A pair of three-tier etageres topped with older male and female figures (emblematic of the hosts?) is shown in Figs. 280-283.

Fig. 276. Two-tier figural sweetmeat étagère (Meissen, c. 1860) with female figure carrying flowers, H 17", Blue Onion pattern (courtesy of the *Doris P. Simonson Collection*).

Fig. 277. Detail of the figure in Fig. 276.

Fig. 279. Detail of the figure in Fig. 278.

Fig. 278. Two-tier figural sweetmeat étagère (Meissen, c. 1860) with male figure carrying a wreath, H 17", Blue Onion pattern, companion piece of the étagère in Fig. 276 (*courtesy of the Doris P. Simonson Collection*).

Fig. 281. Detail of the female figure in Fig. 280, revealing the exquisitely detailed gold and polychrome decoration.

Fig. 280. Three-tier figural sweetmeat étagère (Meissen, c. 1860) with female figure offering flowers, H 17", German Flowers and Insects pattern with original gold trim (estimated value for the matching pair of étagères in Figs. 280 and 282, $2,800-3,000).

Fig. 283. Detail of the male figure in Fig. 282.

Fig. 282. Three-tier figural sweetmeat étagère (Meissen, c. 1860) with male figure toasting the guests, H 17", German Flowers and Insects pattern with original gold trim (see Fig. 280 for value estimate).

There are also objects consisting of a single figure that do not come in pairs, they are mostly putti associated with small baskets engaging in various cooking activities. This series of figurines, not shown here, is known under the name "cupid as cook" (*Amor als Koch*).

The crowning jewel of any blue and white dinner service is the figural centerpiece. As we have seen, its pedigree dates back to the work of Punct during the middle of the eighteenth century. The typical nineteenth century centerpieces consist of a reticulated basket for serving dry sweetmeats or fruits, supported by a stem, with a male and a female figure chasing each other playfully around it. In the example shown in detail in Figs. 284-286, the figures are those of a boy and a girl, the stem consists of a tree stump on a *rocaille* base.

Fig. 284. Centerpiece (Meissen, ca. 1860), boy and girl in playful chase supporting a reticulated basket for the presentation of fruits or dry sweetmeats, applied flowers, Blue Onion pattern in basket interior, H 16", basket L 10.5", W 8" (estimated value $3,000-3,500).

Fig. 286. Interior view of the basket.

Fig. 285. Another view of the centerpiece of Fig. 284

In the following centerpieces of Figs. 287-292 from the Doris P. Simonson Collection, the figures are of young men and women. The stem is a palmetto representing a horn of plenty out of which arises a reticulated basket. Unique about one of the centerpieces is its complete, very labor-intensive floral encrustation.

Fig. 287. Centerpiece (Meissen, c. 1860), couple at play around a palmetto stump supporting a basket, H 19", basket L 13", W 11" (*courtesy of the Doris P. Simonson Collection*).

Fig. 288. Detailed view of the figures on the centerpiece of Fig. 287.

Fig. 289. Another detailed view of the figures on the centerpiece of Fig. 287, focusing on the female figure.

Fig. 290. Monumental Centerpiece (Meissen, c. 1890) with male and female figures around a palmetto stump, H 24", bowl L 14", W 11" (courtesy of the Doris P. Simonson Collection).

Fig. 291. Detail of Fig. 290.

Fig. 292. Detail of Fig. 290.

Another variant shows putti playing musical instruments and leaning against a stem shaped unambiguously as a horn-of-plenty (Figs. 293-294).

Fig. 293. Centerpiece with Musical Putti (Meissen, c. 1860), H 13", bowl L 10", W 7" (courtesy of the Doris P. Simonson Collection).

Fig. 294. Detail of putti in Fig. 293.

The rare centerpiece in Fig. 295 introduces a new theme, that of a mother and her son standing on her lap. This motif is quite unlike other centerpiece motifs with their amorous innuendos. This parent and child motif is more common on figural candelabra that come in pairs. The companion figure to the one shown here is a father with his daughter standing on his lap. A polychrome version of the pair supporting multiple-armed candelabra (with repairs to one candelabrum) recently realized $2,420 at auction.

Opposite page:
Fig. 295. Centerpiece (Meissen, c. 1860), female peasant figure and son standing on her lap at the foot of a palmetto supporting reticulated basket decorated in the Blue Onion pattern, H 16.75", the companion piece has a male peasant figure with daughter striking a similar pose (*courtesy of Auktionshaus Bergmann, Erlangen, Germany*), (estimated value $2,500-3,000).

The final figural shapes we shall consider are the multiple candelabra supported by putti. Candelabra would adorn the dining table or sideboard, typically in pairs, though one might see them offered singly at auctions or antique shows. One such candelabrum with two putti carrying flowers and a wreath is shown in Fig. 296 with a close up of the putti in Fig. 297.

Fig. 296. Figural candelabrum (Meissen, c. 1860) with four lights, allegory of Summer, H 19.75", (*courtesy of Auktionshaus Bergmann, Erlangen, Germany*), (estimated value $2,900-3,300).

Fig. 297. Detail of the figures in Fig. 296.

Fig. 298. Scent bottle (Meissen, c. 1860), extremely rare, dauber with bird finial, in the Blue Onion pattern with original gold trim (*courtesy of the Doris P. Simonson Collection*).

There are also centerpieces and candelabra with groupings of more than two figures. Examples include a rosette-reticulated basket supported by young women emblematic of the three graces, as well as centerpieces and candelabra with three or more putti playing musical instruments. A rare centerpiece has two couples locked in embrace on either side of the stem.

Miscellaneous accessories unrelated to the table: The Meissen Manufactory offered items in underglaze blue unrelated to the dining or dessert table beginning with its first pricelists from ca. 1765. They were listed in the category *Diverses* and included accessories like paperweights shaped as slippers, desk sets comprising inkwells, blotters, and quill trays, toothbrush trays, soap boxes, and bidets. More recent items include letter openers, flowerpots, single candlesticks (which could be used on the table), candleholders, and snuffers for extinguishing the candles. Throughout the eighteenth, nineteenth, and early twentieth centuries these diverse objects comprised about twenty percent of all Blue Onion items listed in the pricelists. In the 1980s the fraction of such objects rose to over thirty percent. A handful of particularly tasteful objects from the middle of the nineteenth century are shown in the following pages (Figs. 298-301).

Fig. 299. Paperweight (Meissen, c. 1860) with Kaendler pug, L 7.88" (courtesy of the Doris P. Simonson Collection).

Fig. 300. Monumental covered urn (Meissen, c. 1860), (courtesy of the Doris P. Simonson Collection).

Fig. 301. Detail of the large floral finial of the urn in Fig. 300.

Novelty items from outside the major manufactories: The so-called Blue Onion craze of the late nineteenth century gave rise to many porcelain as well as non-porcelain novelty items by a very large number of manufacturers and merchandisers. Among the non-porcelain items one finds pottery, metal canisters, napkins, tablecloths, and placemats. These items are of marginal significance to the serious collector and are not included in the present discussion. Two items were selected because they are rather unusual. The lemon press shown in Figs. 302 and 303 has the shape of a stylized bird with its beak as the spout. It is a late nineteenth century German product from an unknown manufacturer. The second item, shown in Fig. 304, is a rare beverage dispenser by the Carl Teichert Manufactory (cf. section on marks) from c. 1890.

Fig. 302. Lemon press (unknown German manufacturer, late 19th century) in the shape of a bird with the beak as spout, L 5.13", (*courtesy of Auktionshaus Bergmann, Erlangen, Germany*), (estimated value $350-450).

Fig. 303. A different view of the lemon press showing its operation.

An example of Blue Onion pottery (as opposed to porcelain) with a creative touch is the bowl made by Villeroy & Boch in their Dresden factory and shown in Figs. 305 and 306. The bowl interior is decorated with the presumptive "onion" unlike the simple Indian floral décor traditionally seen inside Meissen cups.

Fig. 304. Beverage dispenser (Carl Teichert Manufactory, c. 1890) fluted body, original lid with finial, H 14.25" (*courtesy of Auktionshaus Bergmann, Erlangen, Germany*), (estimated value $400-450).

Fig. 305. Bowl (Villeroy & Boch Dresden Factory, late 19th century), Blue Onion decoration on pottery, H 2", D 3.5" (estimated value $25-50).

Fig. 306. Interior of the bowl in Fig. 305 with an unusual single putative "onion" as an independent decorative motif.

Nineteenth Century Sets with Overdecoration

Underglaze blue sets from the nineteenth century that have been overdecorated in the Manufactory consist of the same shapes as the plainer patterns. We have grouped the illustrations of the individual overdecorated pieces by pattern rather than shape to facilitate the comparison of details.

Gold-highlighted Blue Onion Pattern: The gilding of an underglaze blue pattern was a well-established tradition, long before the European invention of hard-paste porcelain. The Chinese bowl of Fig. 15 later gilded and fitted with ormolu mounts in Europe is an example. The gold highlighting (some scholars use the words illumination in analogy to an illuminated manuscript or shading in direct translation of the German *Schattierung*) was perceived as adding value and elegance. The Vine Leaf pattern on the teapot from ca. 1820 shown in Fig. 194 is also highlighted in gold (the pattern is listed in the 1840 catalog as *grüner Weinblätterkranz, die Blätter goldschattiert* or "green vine leaf wreath the leaves shaded in gold" and commands a fifty percent premium in price). It is likely that the gilded version of the Blue Onion pattern became available around the same time.

The extent of gilding varies with the decorator. A relatively early mocha cup and saucer from ca. 1850 shown in Fig. 307 is gilded rather elaborately with thick gold lines outlining the chrysanthemum, the two large leaves, the ledge border, and the fruits. The rectangular covered vegetable dish of Fig. 308 is similarly decorated.

Fig. 307. Mocha cup and saucer (Meissen, c. 1850). Blue Onion pattern highlighted in gold, deep saucer D 4.5", cup D 2.5", H 2.5" total (estimated value $175-200).

Fig. 308. Covered vegetable dish with twisted finial (Meissen, c. 1860). Blue Onion pattern highlighted in gold, L 11", W 8.25", H 6" (courtesy of the Doris P. Simonson Collection).

The gilding of the assorted pieces from a breakfast set shown in Figs. 309-316 is significantly more restrained as is the tureen of Fig. 317.

Fig. 309. Cream jug (Meissen, c. 1860). Blue Onion pattern highlighted in gold, H 5", W 5", part of a four-piece dejeuner set (estimated value for the total set $900-1,100).

Fig. 310. Another view of the cream jug in Fig. 309.

Fig. 311. Sugar bowl with lid (Meissen, c. 1860). Blue Onion pattern highlighted in gold, D 4", H 4.75", part of a four-piece dejeuner set (estimated value for the total set $900-1,100).

Fig. 312. Detail of the lid for the sugar bowl of Fig. 311, showing rosebud finial and gold highlighting.

Fig. 313. Coffeepot (Meissen, c. 1860), Blue Onion pattern highlighted in gold, H 9", W 7", part of a four-piece dejeuner set (estimated value for the total set $900-1,100).

Fig. 314. A different view of the coffeepot in Fig. 313.

Fig. 315. Detail of the lid for the coffeepot of Fig. 313, showing rosebud finial and gold highlighting.

Fig. 316. Deep reticulated serving dish (Meissen, c. 1860), reticulation interrupted by three cartouches, Blue Onion pattern highlighted in gold, D 11", H 2", part of a four-piece dejeuner set (estimated value for the total set $900-1,100).

Fig. 317. Covered tureen with underplate (Meissen, c. 1860), Blue Onion pattern highlighted in gold (*courtesy of the Doris P. Simonson Collection*).

Rich Blue Onion Pattern: Around 1851 Meissen began offering a version of the Blue Onion pattern overdecorated with gold highlighting and rust and coral red foliate ornamentation. The pattern is known as Rich Blue Onion (*rot-gold gehöhtes Zwiebelmuster* or *reiches Zwiebelmuster*). Unlike the sometimes gaudy polychrome *Hausmalerei*, the Meissen overdecoration, when limited to just gold and red, is distinguished by a restrained elegance. The sales volumes of the Rich Blue Onion pattern lagged behind and it was not produced in the same large quantities as the ordinary version. Hence today Rich Blue Onion pieces from the nineteenth century are only moderately obtainable. A selection of Rich Blue Onion items is shown in Figs. 318-330.

Fig. 318. Dessert plate (Meissen, c. 1860), reticulated with three cartouches, Rich Blue Onion pattern, D 8" (estimated value $325-375).

Fig. 319. Luncheon plate (Meissen, c. 1860), Rich Blue Onion pattern, D 8.25" (estimated value $225-275).

Fig. 320. Dinner plate (Meissen, c. 1860), Rich Blue Onion pattern, D 9" (estimated value $225-275).

Fig. 321. Demitasse and saucer (Meissen, c. 1860), Rich Blue Onion pattern, cup H 1.88", D 2.5", saucer D 4" (estimated value $275-300).

Fig. 322. Cup and saucer (Meissen, c. 1860), Rich Blue Onion pattern, cup H 2.25", D 3.25", saucer D 5.13" (estimated value $275-300).

Fig. 323. Teapot (Meissen, c. 1860), Rich Blue Onion pattern, H 8" (estimated value $550-625).

Fig. 324. Frontal view of the teapot in Fig. 323.

Fig. 325. Another side view of the teapot in Fig. 323.

Fig. 326. Plate and silverware (Meissen, c. 1860), Rich Blue Onion pattern, plate 9.75" (*courtesy of a private collection*), (estimated value plate $190-220, silverware handles $80-110 each).

Fig. 327. Covered tureen and underplate (Meissen, c. 1860), Rich Blue Onion pattern, lid with figural finial of a boy holding the mouth of the horn-of-plenty with his right hand, tureen L 15", H 11.25", underplate L 16", W 11.25" (*courtesy of a private collection*), (estimated value $3250-3750).

Fig. 328. Dinner bell (Meissen, c. 1860), Rich Blue Onion pattern (estimated value $300-350), H 4.25", D 2.75" (*courtesy of a private collection*).

Fig. 330. Round covered tureen with underplate (Meissen, c. 1860), lid with figure of a girl holding the mouth of a horn-of-plenty with her left hand, Rich Blue Onion pattern (*courtesy of the Doris P. Simonson Collection*).

Fig. 329. Covered vegetable dish (Meissen, c. 1860), rectangular, lid with twisted finial, Rich Blue Onion pattern, L 11" (courtesy of Auktionshaus Bergmann, Erlangen, Germany), (estimated value $1,100-1,300).

The pattern is still being produced today. A recent example of an egg pan from the year 2000 is shown in Fig. 331 to complete the discussion of shapes associated with eggcups and the serving of eggs.

Fig. 331. Footed egg pan (Meissen, 2000), Rich Onion pattern, factory overdecorated with gold highlighting and rust red embellishments, standing on three volute feet, D 5", H 3.75" (courtesy of Auktionshaus Bergmann, Erlangen, Germany), (estimated value $350-400).

Japanese Garden with Table or Small Table Pattern (*Tischchenmuster*): We have already encountered this pattern in our discussion of unique eighteenth century objects with Imari-inspired decoration. This manner of decoration completes a basic underglaze blue design with polychrome overglaze embellishments. The *Tischchenmuster*, initially one of several Imari or Kakiemon-like patterns, is nevertheless the only one that has been in continuous production since ca. 1732 and has survived virtually unchanged. The Imari-style decoration regained its popularity during the twentieth century and several different patterns, mostly eighteenth century revivals, are offered by Meissen today.

A series of representative examples from a significant private collection can be seen in Figs. 332-341. The pattern is best suited for the decoration of flat surfaces, but it can also be adopted to fit at least partially a curved surface like the footed bowl in Fig. 337, and even a truly irregular shape like a candlestick.

Examples of *Tischchenmuster* from the nineteenth century are rare to moderately obtainable. They were certainly expensive to make, requiring repeated firings at various temperatures (cf. Chapter I of Part I for the chemistry and technology of porcelain) and were only made to order. The artists appear to have had some latitude in painting the pattern. The color palette is not always the same, with differences in the hue and saturation of colors. The manner in which the gold highlighting is applied on the underglaze blue features may also vary from one item to another.

Fig. 332. Large chocolate pot (Meissen, c. 1860), factory overdecorated Japanese Garden with Table (*Tischchenmuster*). H 8.5", W (spout-to-handle) 8" (*courtesy of a private collection*).

Fig. 333. Small chocolate pot (Meissen, c. 1860), factory overdecorated Japanese Garden with Table (*Tischchenmuster*), H 6.25", W (spout-to-handle) 6" (*courtesy of a private collection*).

Fig. 334. Two-compartment salt cellar (Meissen, c. 1860), factory overdecorated Japanese Garden with Table (*Tischchenmuster*), D 2", L 5" (*courtesy of a private collection*).

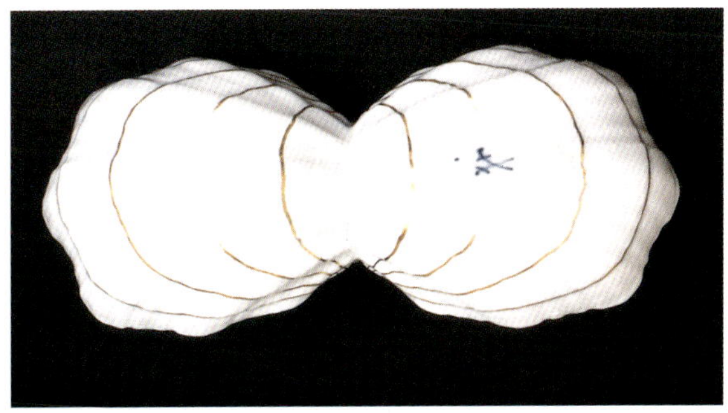

Fig. 335. Another view of the salt cellar in Fig. 334, showing the meticulous gilding of the underside, even though not ordinarily visible when the item is in use.

Fig. 336. Quatrefoil cup and saucer (Meissen, c. 1860), factory overdecorated Japanese Garden with Table (*Tischchenmuster*), saucer L 5.75", W 4.75", cup 3.5" by 2.75" (*courtesy of a private collection*), (estimated value $375-425).

Fig. 337. Footed bowl (Meissen, c. 1860), factory overdecorated Japanese Garden with Table (*Tischchenmuster*), H 6", D 5 3/8" (*courtesy of a private collection*).

Fig. 338. Figural tureen (Meissen, c. 1860), factory overdecorated Japanese Garden with Table (*Tischchenmuster*). H 10", L 12" (*courtesy of a private collection*), (estimated value $3,500-4,000).

Fig. 339. Detail of the finial on the figural tureen of Fig 338 with kneeling girl holding the mouth of the horn-of-plenty with her left hand.

Fig. 340. Detail of the tureen in Fig. 338, showing the adaptation of the pattern to an intricate surface.

Fig. 341. Plateau (Meissen, c. 1860), factory overdecorated Japanese Garden with Table (*Tischchenmuster*), L 16" (*courtesy of a private collection*), (estimated value $1,000-1,500).

Assembling Nineteenth Century Dinner and Dessert Sets

Undoubtedly, one of the most rewarding outcomes of collecting blue and white china is the assembly of complete dinner and/or dessert services. Depending on size and quality such services can be decorative, utilitarian, or investment-grade collections. There are no absolute rules as how a set should be assembled and what follows reflects mostly the author's personal preferences, based on experience.

Meissen Blue Onion pieces from the eighteenth century are generally rare, expensive, and the assortment of shapes is rather limited. They also tend to be one-of-a-kind items with great variability in the design, even when executed by the same artist. Therefore in our opinion eighteenth century Meissen underglaze blue decorated porcelain is not conducive to the creation of entire sets. Such items should be enjoyed individually as cabinet pieces. It is an entirely different matter, of course, if you trace your lineage to Saxon nobility, and happen to have inherited such a set created specifically by special order for one of your ancestors.

The primary criterion for assembling a nineteenth or twentieth century set is consistency, by which we mean uniformity of manufacturer, appearance, period, and color. The second criterion is completeness. Finally, for investment grade sets, the choice of a particular manufacturer is also a significant factor. Blue Onion sets other than by Meissen or KPM Berlin will appreciate in value much more slowly, if at all. On the other hand, one is much more comfortable in treating less expensive sets as utilitarian items that are, in fact, used in the way they were intended. Let us now examine these criteria more closely.

Collectors of dining services should first decide on a manufactory and stick with it. Obviously, Meissen has been the author's preference. Uniformity of shape is also important. As we have already seen, while the Blue Onion pattern was painted on many shapes, it harmonizes best and has reached unsurpassed popularity on the "Neuer Ausschnitt" or "New Cutout" form first designed by Kaendler in 1745. This shape would be the easiest to complete and has evidently withstood the test of time. Another element of appearance is gilding. Mixing plain and gilded pieces in the same set seems offensive to the eye. The same is true of mixing pieces from different periods, especially pre- and post 1888 pieces, since, as we will discuss, in the next chapter, the crossed swords in the later pieces are always repeated also within the pattern itself, and are readily discernible. We would also advise against mixing first and second choice pieces. Assembled Meissen sets, for example, should preferably not contain pieces with incisions across the crossed swords. In short consistency in every respect is worthwhile.

The second criterion is completeness. In the nineteenth century the Meissen Manufactory sold sets for 12, 18, and 24 persons. In the twentieth century sets for 12 were more common. Besides the requisite number of place settings, completeness also entails owning an adequate number of serving pieces. It should be stressed however that for investment grade sets, in addition to the above, an almost complete assortment of all figural pieces of that period would be expected.

A question that inevitably arises is what to do with damaged pieces. Since 1996 Meissen operates a workshop for the repair or restoration of porcelain originally produced by the Manufactory. They claim to use original colors, materials, and designs to reproduce the original appearance of a damaged object (Sonntag 1999(b)). The workshop differentiates between repair and conservation (which they call restoration). Historically significant pieces with damage are simply conserved. In this context conservation implies a minimally invasive procedure that protects the integrity of the item but avoids making irreversible changes, like the removal of any original material or the addition of material that permanently bonds to the surface. Minor chips and scratches or tight hairline cracks are left alone. Most serious conservators would recommend this course of action for rare European porcelain from the early part of the eighteenth century.

Whether extensive repairs to later pieces are worthwhile is a more complex question. Like with all antiques, the value of antique porcelain is typically determined by three factors: rarity, condition and aesthetic appeal. Condition cannot be truly restored because history cannot really be undone, and all repairs are in principle detectable. In other words no amount of repair can recover in full the value lost to damage. A skillful repairer, working from a picture or accurate drawing of the original, can nevertheless bring back the aesthetic appeal of a damaged item. In the case of tableware function can only be partially restored. Repaired utensils should not be exposed to hot water or harsh cleansing agents. Always consult your porcelain conservator for recommendations about the usability of a repaired item. It is certainly worthwhile to repair the mechanism that connects the pieces in items composed of two or more parts such as tazzae or etageres. Such repairs are inobtrusive and do not come into contact with food during use. This is one of the rare instances where almost full value is recovered.

While underglaze decoration is highly durable, gilding and overdecoration are subject to wear. Early gold decoration such as the eighteenth century gold Chinamen by the gilders of Augsburg is best left in an "as is" condition. Even the best conservator ought not to be matching her or his skills against those of the Seuter workshop. The regilding of originally utilitarian pieces is largely a matter of taste and typically gives mixed results. It looks harsh and cheap when viewed against the original elegant background.

PART III

Marks, Copies, and Imitations

Chapter I

Crossed Swords and Other Factory Marks on Meissen's Blue and White Porcelain

"A foolish consistency is the hobgoblin of little minds..." so wrote the American poet Ralph Waldo Emerson. Indeed, in the spirit of that quote there was nothing "little" about the creative minds of the Meissen manufacturists, and that fact was also reflected by their marks. A brief discussion of initials, Roman numerals and other symbols, such as points, lines, and stars, that are found together with the crossed swords on eighteenth century Meissen pieces was already given. Many more details of the Meissen marks have been discussed extensively by Röntgen (Röntgen 1996, Röntgen 2004, Arnold 1989) and also by von Barsewisch (von Barsewisch 1988). The following discussion is based on their insightful scholarship.

The first Meissen marks were actually overglaze marks intended to identify a piece as having been decorated in the manufactory. These marks consisted of letters like M. P. M., K. P. F. or K. P. M. (which in the original eighteenth century German spelling stood for *Meissener Porcelaine-Manufactur, Königliche Porcelaine-Fabrique and Königliche Porcelaine-Manufactur* respectively). Since all underglaze blue painting is by necessity carried out in the Manufactory, these marks do not ordinarily appear on Meissen's blue and white porcelain. Marks that could be used securely to identify the manufacturer's identity first became possible with the development of a controllable process for underglaze blue painting. In general these marks (and this is particularly true of the crossed swords marks) were applied by apprentices and thus there is considerable variability in their shape that cannot be used reliably to determine the age of a piece. A significant exception is the practice of blue painters to mark their own work. As von Barsewisch points out, this custom could in principle make marks like the crossed swords marks as distinctive as the painters' own handwriting. To the best of the author's knowledge, however, no systematic studies of the subject have been published.

Kite Mark and Kite's Tail Mark: The earliest marks on underglaze blue Meissen porcelain are the kite mark (*Drachenmarke*) consisting of a stylized kite in the shape of a crosshatched rhombus with a squiggly line as the tail, and a related mark consisting just of the squiggly line known as the kite's tail mark (*Drachenschwanzmarke*) or whip mark (*Peitschenmarke*). The latter mark has also been interpreted as a caduceus mark. This interpretation is probably erroneous because by historical convention since Antiquity, the caduceus marks should always come in pairs. The central European culture would have been observant of this tradition. The tradition is preserved for example on the well-known mark for Villeroy and Boch. Both the kite and kite's tail marks date to 1722/23. As an example, the kite mark is found (among other objects) on the pear-shaped jug by Johann Christoph Horn (Fig. 26) that was discussed earlier. The kite's tail mark is found on six shallow bowls presented together with thirteen other pieces to August the Strong on February 1722. One of those bowls is in the Gardiner Museum Collection in Toronto and the mark is shown in Fig. 342 below.

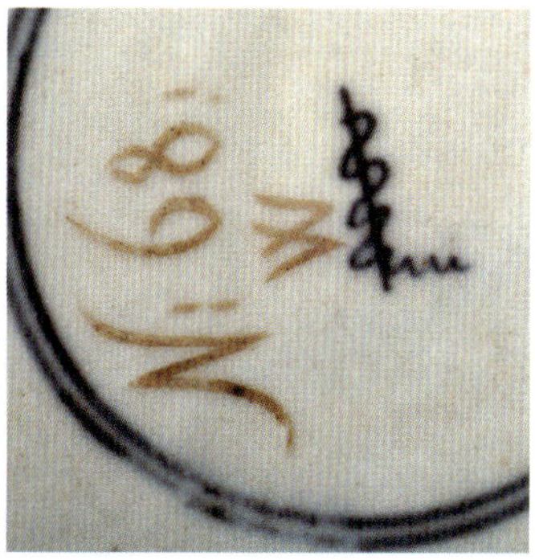

Fig. 342. Kite's tail or whip mark together with the Johanneum number "N 68 W" on the Meissen saucer from 1721 shown in Fig. 28 *(reproduced with permission, The Gardiner Museum of Ceramic Art, Toronto Canada).*

The use of the kite's tail mark continued even after the crossed swords marks were formally introduced by a royal decree in 1729. The reason for this is what we might consider today as multicultural sensitivity. The officially Moslem Ottoman Empire was one of Meissen's largest and most lucrative markets, a market in which the Manufactory competed with Chinese porcelain. In fact the Ottoman Turks imported tea bowls in such quantities that these objects have come to be known as "Turkish tea bowls" or *Türkenkoppchen*. The Moslem rulers objected to the crossed swords as being reminiscent of Christian crosses, a symbol unacceptable to them. Following arduous negotiations, the kite's tail mark was continued on ware destined for the Ottoman Empire. Curiously the trade representative for the Ottoman Court conducting negotiations with the Manufactory was a Christian, the Greek merchant Athanasios Manassas. This was in keeping with the Ottoman Empire's tradition of being represented diplomatically and commercially in Europe by its Greek subjects.

Marks with Pseudo-Chinese Characters: An equally early mark is a set of meaningless symbols imitating Chinese ideograms. There can be up to six of them typically arranged in three rows of two. A shallow plate by Horn displays three such characters in combination with the kite's tail mark. Later these marks, too, became a substitute for crossed swords on wares intended for the Moslem world. An often-cited example is a tea bowl with underglaze green pseudo-Chinese characters that had to have been marked after 1817 (see discussion of nineteenth century technical innovations).

The Intertwined AR Mark: This is probably one of the most copied, imitated, and forged marks in the history of porcelain. The initials AR in intertwined script stand for Augustus Rex, Latin for August the King, and were initially meant for porcelain intended for the Royal Court. As marks they appear on very large vases intended for King August's personal collection in his Porcelain Palace (for an example cf. color plate on p. 197 in Arnold 1989). They also appear on underglaze blue tableware as part of the decoration.

The Underglaze Blue Crossed Swords Mark: The crossed swords mark is the quintessential feature of Meissen porcelain. It has been imitated countless times by lesser manufactories in the hope of confusing and deceiving novice collectors. Thorough familiarity with all of the legitimate variants of this mark and its imitations is a *conditio sine qua non* of being a serious porcelain collector.

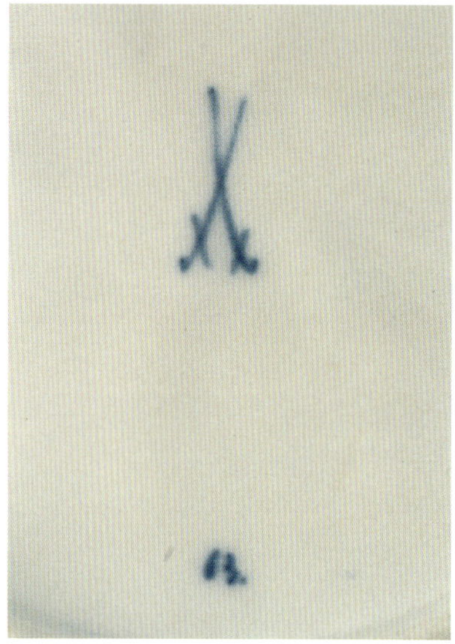

Fig. 343. Mark on the royal blue centerpiece of Fig. 4, mid-19th century.

The exact date for the introduction of the crossed swords mark is not recorded in the Manufactory Archives. In 1722, inspector Steinbrück proposed the use of the crossed swords, part of the Saxon coat-of-arms as the Manufactory mark. Beyond being mere symbols of the Prince Elector, the crossed swords also signified the fact that the Electors of Saxony were Grand Marshals of the Empire (*Reichserzmarschall*), a title second only to that of German Emperor. The coat-of-arms with the swords can be seen right over one of the majestic gates leaving the Zwinger courtyard (Fig. 24). The swords were "in common use" by 1728, but the royal decree directing their use was first issued formally in 1729.

The reader may have already noticed the tremendous variability in the crossed swords marks, even on pieces from the same era. Marcolini period (1774-1814) swords, for example, might have no pommels at all, or pommels in the shape of a dot (*Knaufschwerter*), or a short dash (sometimes referred to as *Strichschwerter*). The hilts on such swords might be represented by straight or wavy lines. The articles and books by Robert Röntgen are an excellent source of information on this subject. Still, the best way for collectors to educate themselves is to examine the marks on Meissen porcelain (and that of the other significant manufacturers we will discuss), in museums, and serious galleries or at the previews of high-end auctions.

During the second quarter of the nineteenth century the swords were applied sloppily or tended to flow because of the chemical composition and consistency of the clay body prior to firing. These swords appear "smeared," and this period in the history of the Manufactory is known as the "Smeared Marks Period" or *Schmierzeit*. Later in the nineteenth century the swords assumed a certain curvature and the pommels migrated towards the outside of the handles as shown in Fig. 343. After 1924 the pommels were dropped altogether.

One final point concerns the location of the swords within the design. Typically they are found on the underside of an object. But this is not the only place. On at least two teapots dating to around 1730-40, one in the Dresden porcelain collection and one in the author's possession, the crossed swords mark is found at the base of the handle. This mark is shown in Fig. 99. There are of course also objects without a natural "underside" such as porcelain handles for silverware, ink-blotters, and knobs of all kinds. In such objects the crossed swords mark is by necessity on the side of the object exposed to normal viewing.

Starting ca. 1888 Meissen began to incorporate the crossed swords mark into various underglaze blue patterns in order to protect itself against imitators. In the case of the Blue Onion pattern the mark appears at the base of the bamboo tree since 1888 as shown in Figs. 344-347. After ca. 1890 (Sterba 1988), it also appears on the "rock" of the Rock and Bird pattern. Finally, just a few years ago, when Meissen rediscovered the popularity of the Strawflower pattern and started producing it again, they placed the crossed swords also on the front as part of the decoration. While providing some visual reinforcement that the item in question is indeed authentic and not a cheap imitation, this practice is esthetically speaking rather unappealing. It serves to date pieces quickly and has the unintended but beneficial consequence of excluding relatively recent pieces from assembled mid-nineteenth century dinner services.

Fig. 344. Post-1888 crossed swords mark as it appears at the base of the bamboo tree in the Blue Onion pattern.

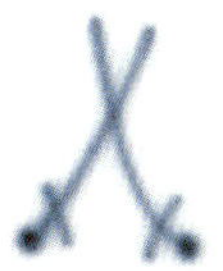

Fig. 345. Post-1888 crossed swords mark on the underside of the plate shown in Fig. 344.

Fig. 346. Post-1934 crossed swords mark as it appears at the base of the bamboo tree in the Blue Onion pattern.

Fig. 347. Post-1934 crossed swords mark on the underside of the vase shown in Fig. 346.

This practice, however, is by no means universal. A revival of the early eighteenth century three-fruit variant of the Blue Onion pattern, known as "Original Blue Onion after Dr. Spitzner" (*Original Zwiebelmuster nach Dr. Spitzner*) introduced around 1880 and still in production after WW II, **does not include the crossed swords at the foot of the bamboo tree even on post 1888 pieces!** The crossed swords and other markings on the underside of such items are, nevertheless, consistent with the marking practices at the time of production.

Incisions and Quality Control: Incisions, that is markings cut through the glaze with a cutter's wheel, near or across the crossed swords mark are often the source of confusion and not only for beginner collectors. The source of the confusion is that incisions address two different issues, quality and authorship of the decoration. Since sometime before 1764 **one incision *across* the swords** was used **on porcelain sold undecorated** and **has no implications as to the quality** of the object. Any **overglaze decoration on porcelain bearing a singly incised mark was definitely applied outside the Meissen Manufactory.** We should note parenthetically that **the converse of this statement is not true. Absence of an incision does not mean that *all* of the overglaze decoration was completed in the Manufactory.** Since the blue decoration we are concerned with in this book is underglaze decoration, marks with a single incision are of no further concern.

After 1852 incisions were also used to signify the quality grade of porcelain. Two quality grades were already mentioned by Inspector Steinbrück as early as 1712. Over the next hundred years the number of quality grades fluctuated between six and four. In 1852 second, third, and fourth choice overglaze decorated porcelain was marked with two, three, and four incisions respectively across the crossed swords. The system was extended to blue and green underglaze decorated porcelain in 1853. In the latter case however, the quality marks were either horizontal incisions above or vertical incisions to the left or to the right of the crossed swords mark. From 1869-1980 the incisions were placed across the crossed swords even for underglaze decorated ware. This convention changed in 1980 and again in 1986. These last changes are of no significance to an antiques collector and the interested reader is referred to the treatise by Röntgen (Röntgen 1996).

Underglaze Blue Dots, Circles, Lines, and Stars in Association with the Crossed Swords: Starting around 1730 until well into the latter part of the eighteenth century, a single dot between the hilts or a circle between the blades can be found. Contemporary research contradicts the earlier notion of the existence of a well-defined "Dot Period." There are certainly no published reports of official decrees declaring the commencement or termination of this practice.

Somewhat more useful in dating objects are the marks introduced during the directorship of Count Camillo Marcolini (years of service: 1774-1814). During 1774, the first year of Marcolini's directorship, a vertical underglaze blue line placed under the crossed swords was used, or alternatively, two dots with one dot above the other. The latter variant however has also been observed on objects from 1725-1750, both in the von Barsewisch collection as well as in the Syz collection (see Fig. 94). The following year Marcolini ordered the use of an underglaze blue star under the crossed swords mark. This combination was in use from 1775 to 1814 and lingered on until probably 1817.

A dot between the blades of contemporary curved swords without pommels was used during 1924-1934 under the directorship of Max Adolf Pfeiffer. This mark, which can be used to date early twentieth century pieces rather narrowly, is known as the Pfeiffer mark (*Pfeiffermarke*).

A single underglaze blue line, located away from the crossed swords and close to the foot rim, was added in 1953 as a date mark. The date correlation is as follows: 1953-57 vertical line under the swords, 1957-72 horizontal line under the swords, 1972-80 vertical line to the right of the swords, 1980 horizontal line to the right of the swords, since 1980 horizontal line to the left of the swords. An example including incisions for second choice is shown in Fig. 348.

Fig. 348. Crossed swords and date mark for 1980 second choice ware on the plate shown in Fig. 5.

Impressed Marks: During the early years of the Manufactory, throwers and molders impressed their signs on white ware in a rather arbitrary and capricious manner. A table associating these marks with individual throwers or molders has been given by many authors, it can be found most readily in Röntgen (Röntgen 1996). By 1739 Kaendler compiled an inventory of these marks and proposed that they be substituted by impressed numbers. Thus numbers impressed into the porcelain appear after 1740. These numbers cannot be correlated with dates, since the Manufactory has not revealed this information. Some blue and white Meissen pieces from the third quarter of the eighteenth century (one now in the Syz Collection) display an impressed mark similar in shape to an Irish cross, also known as a cross "*formee*". Its significance is not clear, and it has not been discussed by Röntgen.

Other impressed marks signify shape numbers and (after 1948) the year of production.The letter B was impressed on tableware to be painted blue on orders of Director Camillo Marcolini issued in 1804. This practice may have continued as late as 1817.

Underglaze Blue Painters' Marks: These include letters, dots, Roman numerals, and numbers, all in underglaze blue and applied by the blue painter's hand. We have already discussed letters as possibly initials of blue painters in conjunction with individual eighteenth century pieces. Other symbols include three dots defining a triangle, crosses, crescents, squares, bows, and an arrow pointing towards a dot (rare, cf. von Barsewisch 1988). A commonly recurring Roman numeral is "XI." All of these symbolic marks defy any plausible interpretation. It is possible that many of the painters were illiterate and could not mark their work with letters.

At some point during the middle of the eighteenth century, the initials migrated to the foot rim and subsequently gave way to painters' numerals also applied in underglaze blue. An exact date for this transition cannot be given, probably because the archival material from the time of the Seven Years' War (1756-63) has disappeared. Again, there are no lists correlating painters with painters' numerals, consistent with Meissen's desire to maintain the anonymity of its artists.

Overglaze Letters and Numbers in Script: Overglaze groupings of script letters, sometimes with numbers, are inventory marks. Some blue and white tableware from the Warsaw Residence, used prior to 1763, bear a mark with the letters KHCW, which stood for the Royal Court Confectionery, Warsaw or *Königliche Hof-Conditorei Warschau*. The mark on a plate from ca. 1745 discussed earlier is shown in Fig. 349.

Fig. 349. Mark on plate of Fig. 124. Note blue painter's mark and inventory mark K.H.C.W. for Königliche Hof Conditorei Warschau, indicating it belonged to the inventory of the Royal Confectionary at the Warsaw Palace, impressed number 67, four incised vertical lines at the foot rim, incision unrelated to quality (*Courtesy of the Dr. B. von Barsewisch Collection/Schlossmuseum Wolfshagen Prignitz*).

Another marking, not applied in the Manufactory and also found on non-Meissen objects are the so-called Johanneum Numbers. These are inventory numbers of the Royal Porcelain Collection in Dresden. They are either applied in black ink or incised and are supposed to document eighteenth century royal provenance. They are found on Meissen as well as Oriental porcelain. Two examples of this mark were already encountered in Figs. 59 and 342.

Roman Numerals in Association with Nineteenth Century Crossed Swords Marks: For a brief period of time, 1817 to 1824, the Roman numerals I and II in underglaze blue placed directly under the crossed swords were used to signify porcelain made from first or second quality paste. The latter porcelain body was made from lower grades of kaolin from Kaschka and Seilitz. Until 1820 all underglaze blue and green decorated items were made out of the second grade material and marked with the Roman numeral II. This included high-end pieces that received further gilding and overdecoration, like the teapot of Fig. 194. That is the reason we have dated it so narrowly to 1817-1820. The mark is shown in Fig. 350. To the right of the swords one also sees an underglaze green painter's mark "/" together with a script "G" below it. This mark is very similar to the mark of a blue painter known to have been active during the (immediately preceding) Marcolini period. The observation is consistent with the archival records telling us that during this time all underglaze painters were placed together in a single group.

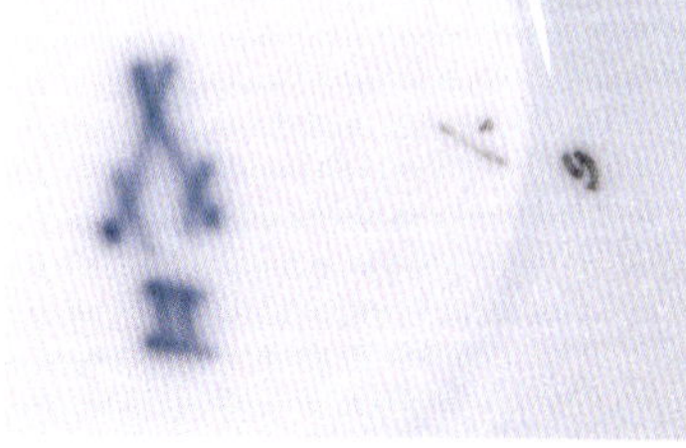

Fig. 350. Mark on teapot of Fig. 195, crossed swords with pommels over Latin numeral II indicative of a lower-grade paste in underglaze blue, also painter's mark "/" and script "G" in underglaze green (early).

Chapter II

Marks of Other Major Manufactories on Similar Eighteenth and Nineteenth Century Blue and White Porcelain

Many of the design elements on Meissen underglaze blue decorated porcelain were quickly adopted by the other major porcelain manufactories of the eighteenth century. We have already seen examples by the Royal Porcelain Manufactories of Berlin, Vienna, and Copenhagen. The designs spread even to minor porcelain factories and to the many faience and pottery decorators, who already had experience in blue and white decoration. The fascination with Chinoiserie was not limited to continental Europe. Early English soft-paste porcelain pieces from Lime House, Lund, and Bow bring small fortunes at auction. A comprehensive treatment of all of these topics in a single volume is clearly not feasible. The other manufactories most likely to be of interest to the American collector of Meissen underglaze blue decorated porcelain are the Royal Porcelain Manufactory (KPM) in Berlin, the Royal Manufactory in Vienna (Royal Vienna), and Royal Copenhagen. We shall restrict ourselves to discussing the details of marks from these three companies, only.

The Royal Vienna Porcelain Manufactory: The best known trade mark of the Vienna Porcelain Manufactory is the shield mark, the *Bindenschildmarke* taken from the coat of arms of the Hapsburgers, the ruling family of the Holy Roman Empire. It was introduced as an impressed mark possibly as early as 1744 (but according to a 1798 report by Director Conrad Sörgel von Sorgenthal in underglaze blue only after 1749) and was in use until 1864 when the manufactory was dissolved. The shape of the mark has been misinterpreted in the Anglo-Saxon world, and is erroneously referred to as the "beehive mark." The mark does indeed have a fleeting resemblance to a beehive, when viewed upside down (!). Imitators have capitalized on this error, and have embellished the "beehive" with a little opening, and even a bee sitting on top of it. These marks are too crude to even be called forgeries. Any writings such as titles and descriptions or other markings that force the mark to be viewed like a beehive are incontrovertible evidence that the object is not authentic, and is made to deceive. An extensive discussion of the Royal Vienna marks is outside the scope of this book. Only those aspects that are relevant to blue and white porcelain will be summarized here as given by Neuwirth (Neuwirth 1982).

a) The blue Hapsburg shield mark must be hand-painted (therefore asymmetric or irregular) and under the glaze.
b) The blue painter numbers applied under the glaze may range only from 1 through 27.
c) The impressed thrower and molder numbers may range only from 1 through 60.

Impressed date marks were introduced by Sorgenthal in 1784 and may range from 84 through 99 for the years 1784-1799 and from 800 through 864 for the years 1800-1864.
Currently known stamped shape numbers reach into the 300s.

Representative early examples of true Royal Vienna marks are shown in Figs. 351 and 352.

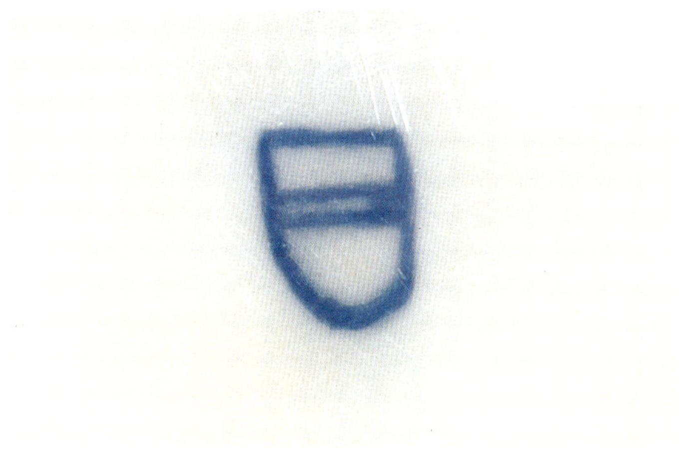

Fig. 351. Royal Vienna mark of the Habsburg shield in underglaze blue on the underside of the plate of Fig. 112 (*Courtesy of the Dr. B. von Barsewisch Collection/Schlossmuseum Wolfshagen Prignitz*).

Fig. 352. Mark of the Royal Vienna Manufactory on the coffeepot of Fig. 101, Habsburg shield mark (*Bindenschild*) in underglaze blue, impressed date mark for 1808. The blue painter's cipher insures that the mark is viewed as a shield, not as a "beehive". The "beehive" mark, though sometimes found on exquisitely painted late 19th century Austrian porcelain, should generally be regarded as a crude imitation of the true Royal Vienna mark shown here.

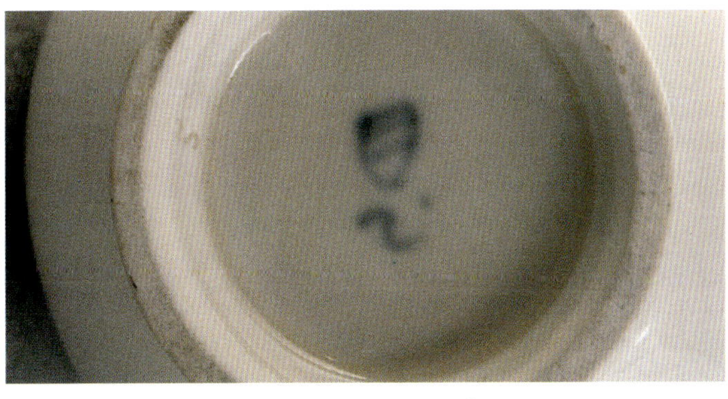

The Royal Berlin Manufactory and its Predecessor Companies: The first successful Prussian porcelain company was founded by Wilhelm Caspar Wegely in 1751 and confirmed by Friedrich the Great on August 2, 1753. The company remained in business until 1757, and has produced blue and white porcelain, primarily in the German flowers and insects pattern. The mark of this factory is the capital letter "W" in underglaze blue or impressed.

A second factory was started in 1761 by Johann Ernst Gotzkowsky which transferred to the king's possession in 1763 thus giving rise to the Royal Porcelain Manufactory Berlin known internationally by its German initials KPM (*Königliche Porzellan Manufaktur*). After WW I and the end of the German monarchy the manufactory was technically called the State Porcelain Manufactory (*Staatliche Porzellan Manufaktur*) but the initials KPM were retained in the mark, reflecting its strong brand name recognition.

The most widely recognized KPM mark is the underglaze blue scepter mark (*Szeptermarke*), a royal symbol in use since ca. 1760 (Baer 1980). The details of the scepter mark have changed over the centuries. The initials "KPM", also in underglaze blue, appear under the scepter mark beginning sometime in the nineteenth century. Another nineteenth century underglaze mark is that of the imperial eagle (*Reichsadlermarke*). Factory decorated pieces also bear the decorating mark with the imperial orb (*Reichsapfel*) and the initials "KPM" in red. Finally for a relatively short time the eagle mark within two concentric circles was used, with the inscription *Koenigl. Porzellan Manufactur* appearing in the space between the two circles. This mark is known as the "penny mark" (*Pfennigmarke*). It was in use 1847-1849 and in conjunction with the scepter mark 1849-1870. An example of the scepter mark is shown in Fig. 353.

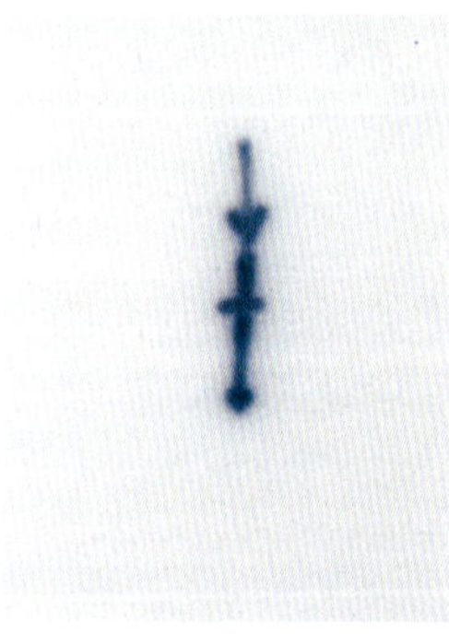

Fig. 353. Mark on the plate of Fig. 95, 18th century scepter mark of the Royal Porcelain Manufactory (KPM) Berlin.

Royal Copenhagen: There were several early unsuccessful attempts to manufacture porcelain in Copenhagen. Between about 1761 and 1766 Louis Fournier (active 1747-74), who had previously worked at Vincennes and Chantilly, directed a factory in Copenhagen that produced soft-paste porcelain. His successor, Franz Heinrich Müller (1732-1820), successfully made hard-paste porcelain by 1773 and founded a company in 1774. Shares in the company were owned by the royal family. In 1779 the company was taken over completely by Christian VII, king of Denmark (1749-1808), and was renamed the Royal Danish Porcelain Factory. It remains in operation today. The basic mark of the Royal Copenhagen factory is three wavy lines in underglaze blue representing Lille Bælt, Store Bælt, and Øresund, the three main waterways that cut through Denmark. The three wavy lines have been retained throughout the history of the manufactory. This basic mark was used from the beginning until 1894. In 1894 the crown and the word "Danmark" were added. In 1898 the mark was changed to Royal Copenhagen with a crown in green and without reference to the country of origin. In 1923 the word "Denmark" was added. After 1935 a systematic dating system was adopted (cf. Pope 2001). Painter's numerals were changed to low case initials around 1928. Representative marks are shown in Figs. 354 and 355 and also in the insert of Fig. 123.

Fig. 354. Mark on the plate of Fig. 121, with underglaze blue wavy lines, crown, and the word "Danmark" in use 1894-1898.

Fig. 355. Mark on the dish of Fig. 122 with crown, Royal Copenhagen and painter's numeral but without country of origin (Denmark), dating the piece to 1898-1923.

Chapter III

Eighteenth Century Forgeries, Nineteenth Century Imitations, and Crude Deceptions

The tremendous popularity of the Blue Onion pattern gave rise to numerous imitations that began appearing during the last quarter of the nineteenth century and continue to be produced even today. Most of these items are easily recognized as new and not from Meissen or the other major manufactories. They are marked as Blue Onion, *Oignon Bleu*, or *Zwiebelmuster* or even with fanciful names like Blue Danube, Nordic Blue, Ming Tree, Vienna Woods, Mimosa French Onion, etc. Any containers with English wording on them, such as "oil," "vinegar," "flour" etc., are also, without exception, imitations that should be avoided by collectors who aspire to assembling serious collections. Röntgen has dealt expertly with most of these issues in his books, and they do not warrant any further detailed discussion here. Instead of repeating Röntgen's incisive analysis, this chapter will concentrate primarily on certain deceptive marks and practices that are still used to mislead novice and in some cases even experienced collectors. Nevertheless, the Teichert marks continue to bedevil collectors and dealers alike and will be mentioned briefly.

Thuringian imitations and forgeries: Fifty years after Bottger's legendary success in the dungeons of the *Jungfernbastei*, European porcelain was allegedly reinvented, this time on three separate occasions in the southeastern German state of Thuringia (*Thüringen*). The names of Georg Heinrich Macheleid, Johann Gotthelf Greiner, and Johann Wolfgang Hammann are associated with the rise of the Thuringian porcelain industry. An extensive discussion of Thuringian porcelain is clearly outside the scope of this book (for an excellent discussion cf. Scherf 1980). Suffice it to say that unlike the manufactories of Meissen, Vienna, and Berlin, these smaller enterprises produced utilitarian ware and figurines for the working classes. Their products can in some ways be compared to those of Staffordshire. Thuringian porcelain is collectible and can be found in museums. Unfortunately the Thuringian manufactories often marked their ware with marks that are very misleading, if not outright forgeries.

Some of the more problematic marks are those of the Volkstedt manufactory (established in Sitzendorf 1760, moved to Volkstedt 1762). Fig. 356 shows the mark on the teapot shown previously in Fig. 120. This is a typical example of an imitation of the Meissen marks by a Thuringian manufactory, most likely Volkstedt.

The pattern on question in most of the Thuringian imitations is the Strawflower. Usually it is painted in a coarse manner, certainly not as a labor of love. The glaze is often defect-ridden to the point that segments of the underlying pattern are washed out.

The mark of the Wallendorf factory (established 1764) is an underglaze blue "W" which has morphed into a pair of crossed checkmarks that could be interpreted as crossed swords. The letter is also reminiscent of the mark of the Wegely manufactory, the first of the Berlin manufactories. The crossed "L"'s of the Limbach factory (established 1772) were drawn in a way that imitates the Meissen mark, especially when a star is added underneath to emulate the Marcolini period crossed swords. The factory in Ilmenau (established 1777) used an underglaze blue vertical line, presumably representing the letter "I" which might be mistaken for the scepter mark of KPM Berlin. The Gera factory (established 1779) mark "G" could be represented as that of the Gotzkowsky manufactory, immediate predecessor of KPM Berlin.

Fig. 356. Imitation crossed swords mark on teapot of Fig. 120, probably from the Volkstedt manufactory in Thuringia.

Despite everything that has been said, eighteenth century Thuringian porcelain items are still important historical documents and deserve scholarly study. It is in no way the intent of the author to detract from their artistic value.

Nineteenth century/early twentieth century marks bearing the words "Meissen" or "Dresden": A quick and cheap way to confuse a novice collector is to include suggestive or misleading words into the marks, like the two magic words, Meissen and Dresden. Examples are shown in Figs. 357-359.

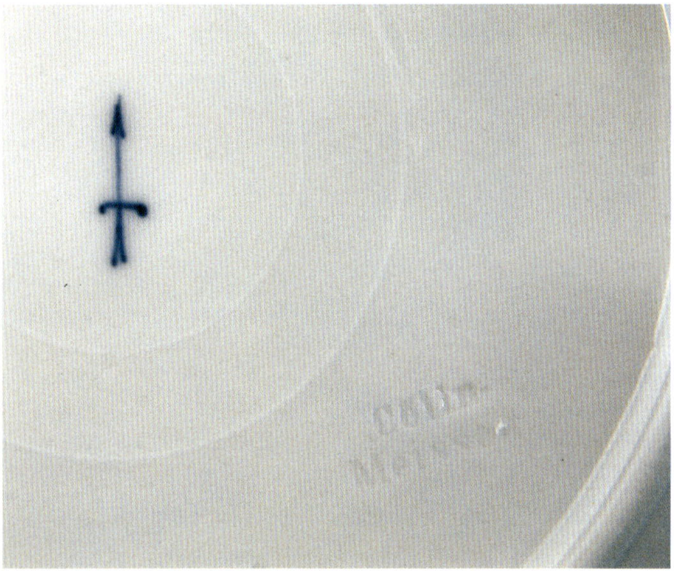

Fig. 357. Mark of the Ernst Teichert Factory found on imitations of the Blue Onion pattern, underglaze blue arrow with impressed Cölln-Meissen 1885-1900, with the word "Meissen" in capital letters as part of the blue mark 1900-1913, with only the letter "M" capitalized 1913-1923.

Fig. 358. Mark of the Carl Teichert Factory found on imitations of the Blue Onion pattern, c. 1885, an oval encircling "Meissen" in capital letters over an asterisk, all in underglaze blue, also impressed "MEISSEN".

Fig. 359. Villeroy & Boch Dresden, mark on bowl of Fig. 305.

Crude deceptions: Finally a word of caution is in order for novice collectors and casual buyers. The crossed swords mark is always applied in blue and under the glaze or on occasion on unglazed bottoms. The marks of the Vienna, Berlin, and Copenhagen manufactories are also in underglaze blue. Overglaze decorator's marks are obviously outside the scope of this book. Be very wary of crude deceptions, like unscrupulous dealers or auctioneers drawing the mark with blue felt tip pens and sometimes covering it under a high-gloss plastic overcoat like nail polish or clear polyurethane. Such forgeries can in principle be exposed using mild organic solvents, a process best left to expert and trustworthy restorers. As a general rule of thumb avoid acquiring allegedly significant and expensive pieces attributed to any manufactory (not just Meissen) with visible alterations in the general area of the marks.

Attempts to mislead using genuine Meissen products: As mentioned previously, during the last quarter of the nineteenth century the Meissen Manufactory attempted to expand interest in the Blue Onion line by introducing several variants of the pattern. One particular variant, the so called "Original Blue Onion Pattern after Dr. Spitzner" (*Original Zwiebelmuster nach Dr. Spitzner*) that went into production around 1880 and was still being produced after WW II, is a copy of the eighteenth century three-fruit variant of the pattern. It does not have the crossed swords repeated in the pattern at the foot of the bamboo tree, and therefore cannot be dated simply by inspection. There are reports of unscrupulous dealers making misleading statements about the age of such pieces trying to represent them as being "possibly of the period." There are some hints to watch for, however. Many (unfortunately not all) "Original Blue Onion" pieces were issued on the New Cutout (*Neuer Ausschnitt*) form, a shape produced at least a decade after the three-fruit variant had given way to the traditional Blue Onion pattern. The painting is very crisp, unlike what one might expect for early eighteenth century items. The objects are marked with the crossed swords in use at the time of production and can help date them to the nineteenth and twentieth centuries. Furthermore, the product line is identified by the decoration number 3a.

Another attempt at misleading novice collectors while using genuine Meissen parts is the assembly of figural etageres from reticulated dessert plates drilled through the middle and "spare" figurines from broken pieces. These marriages can be spotted rather easily. The undersides of the reticulated levels of the etageres are always decorated. The undersides of dessert plates are left blank. In a more blatant example, a recent Internet auction offered a total fantasy piece where a figurine from a broken étagère was attached to the center of a footed bowl. When dealing with items made of two or more pieces, it is generally a good idea to verify that each individual piece is marked with the crossed swords mark. An example is the underside of a tazza shown in Fig. 360. The upper (plate) part of the tazza is marked off-center making it clear that it was intended for mounting on a pedestal.

This rule is not entirely without exceptions. The upper part of the shorter tazza in Fig. 248 bears no visible mark. However both the plate and the pedestal are marked with the same blue painter's numeral near the foot rim, sufficient to document authenticity.

The best way collectors can avoid deception is to visit as many museums, galleries and auctions as possible and acquaint themselves with reliably authenticated pieces. Another good though rare source of information is Meissen's catalogues from the eighteenth and nineteenth centuries.

Fig. 360. View of the underside. A tazza consists of two pieces, held together with an interlocking mechanism. Both parts are marked with underglaze blue crossed swords with 19th century pommels and different blue painter's marks. Note underside decoration that distinguishes the upper piece from a plate of the same size.

Concluding Remarks

Our story of Meissen's underglaze blue porcelain ends in 1896. That year a young but very promising modeler, Julius Konrad Hentschel, designed the highly acclaimed Breakfast Set in the Crocus Pattern (*Krokus-Dejeuner*). Its enthusiastic reception at the 1900 World's Fair in Paris marks the beginning of Meissen's entry into the Art Nouveau era. While the story told here ends with 1896, that date is by no means the end of the whole story! Underglaze blue painted porcelain continued to be a medium of artistic expression for the flowing organic designs of the Art Nouveau, the bold shapes of the Art Deco, and the daring visions of the Moderne. To do them justice would require expanding the scope of this book beyond what is practicable. It is best left as a task for the future.

Fig. 361. Child drinking from Blue Onion cup (Meissen after 1950), original modeled in 1905 by Konrad Hentschel, (estimated value $2,750-3,000 for period piece).

Bibliography

Arnold, Klaus-Peter and Verena Diefenbach. *Meissener Blaumalerei aus drei Jahrhunderten*. Leipzig: 1989.

Baer, Winfried. *Berlin Porcelain*. Washington, D.C.: Smithsonian Institution Press, 1980.

Berling, Karl. *Festive Publication to Commemorate the 200th Jubilee of the Oldest European China Manufactory, Meissen*. (English translation of the *Festschrift zur 200jährigen Jubelfeier der ältesten europäischen Porzellanmanufaktur Meißen 1910*.) Leipzig 1911, reissued by New York: Dover Books, 1972.

Burton, William. *Porcelain, Its Art and Manufacture*. B. T. Batsford, 1906.

Clunas, Craig. *Chinese Export Art and Design*. Kent: Westerham Press, Ltd., 1987.

Cox, Warren E. *The Book of Pottery and Porcelain*. New York, 1945.

Doenges, Willy. *Meissner Porzellan. Seine Geschichte und Künstlerische Entwicklung*. Dresden, 1921.

Eberlein, Harold D. and Cortland V. D. Hubbard. "Ice Cream Jars." *The Magazine Antiques*, August 1950.

Glanville, Philippa and Hilary Young (Eds.). *Elegant Dining; Four Hundred Years of Dining in Style*. London: 2002.

Gleeson, Janet. *The Arcanum*. New York: 1998.

Hesni, Deloris. *The H. Lloyd Hawkins, Jr. Meissen Collection*. New Orleans: 1997.

Honey, W. B. "European Porcelain of the Eighteenth Century." *The Magazine Antiques*, January 1962.

Karpinski, Jürgen. *Schöne Dekore auf Meissener Porzellan*. Leipzig: 2001.

Lebel, Antoine. "Eighteenth Century Chinese Export Porcelain for the French Market." *The Magazine Antiques*, March 2005.

McKearin, Helen. "Sweetmeats in Splendor." *The Magazine Antiques*, March 1955.

Miedtank, Lutz. *Zwiebelmuster*. 3rd Ed. Leipzig: 2001.

Miedtank, Lutz and Sebastian Miedtank. *Wahre Geschichten um das Zwiebelmuster*. Taucha: 2003.

Mields, M. and R. Lauschke. *Praxis der Porzellanmalerei*. Leipzig: 1965.

Neuwirth, Waltraud. *Wiener Porzellan 1718-1864*. Staatliche Museen zu Berlin, 1982.

Reiff, Hermann. "Unterglasurblaue Chinoiserien nach Höroldt-Vorlagen." *Keramos* vol. 111, 1986, pp. 19-26.

Röntgen, Robert E. *The Book of Meissen*, 2nd Ed. Atglen, Pennsylvania: Schiffer Publishing, 1996.

Röntgen, Robert E. *Marks on German, Bohemian and Austrian Porcelain*. Atglen, Pennsylvania: Schiffer Publishing, 1997.

Röntgen, Robert E. *Blaumalerei auf Meissener Porzellan*. Leipzig: 2004.

Rückert, Reiner. *Biographische Daten der Meißener Manufakturisten des 18. Jahrhunderts*, Bayerisches Nationalmuseum, München: 1990.

Savage, George. *Eighteenth Century German Porcelain*. London: 1958.

Scherf, Helmut and Jürgen Karpinski. *Thüringer Porzellan*. Leipzig: 1980.

Sonntag, Hans and Jürgen Karpinski. *Meißener Porzellan; Schönheit im Detail*. Leipzig: 1998.

Sonntag, Hans. *Die Botschaft des Drachen*. Leipzig: 1999(a).

Sonntag, Hans. *Meissen in Meißen*. Leipzig: 1999(b).

Stella, Jacques. *Les jeux et plaisirs de l' enfance* 1657, published as "Games and Pastimes of Childhood," New York: Dover, 1969.

Sterba, Günther. "Zur Entwicklung des Meissner Zwiebelmusters." *Keramos* vol. 111, 1986, pp. 13-18.

Sterba, Günther. *Meißener Tafelgeschirr*. Stuttgart: 1989.

Stümpfle-Wolf, Helene. „Das Bayerische Porzellanschloss." *Trödler u. Sammler Journal*, February 2005, p. 40. The hidden PES initials have also been discussed by Rückert, Rainer. *Meißener Porzellan 1710-1810. Ausstellung im Bayerischen Nationalmuseum München*. Munich: 1966.

Syz, Hans, J. Jefferson Miller, and Rueckert Rainer. *Catalogue of the Hans Syz Collection*. Washington, D.C.: Smithsonian Institution Press, 1979.

Tippett, Paul. *Blue and White China, The Connoisseur's Guide*, published as part of the series "Christie's Collectables." London: 1997.

Von Barsewisch, Bernhard. "Unterglasurblaue Malerei." *Keramos* vol. 121, 1988, pp. 3-201.

Von Barsewisch, Bernhard and Arnulf Stößel. *Keramiken des Bayerischen Nationalmuseums im Internationalen Keramik-Museum Weiden*. Munich: 1990.

Walcha, Otto. "Kleine Chronik der Frühen Meissner Blaumalerei." *Keramos* vol. 47, 1970, pp. 28-35.

Ware, George. *German and Austrian Porcelain*. Frankfurt.

Warren, Phelps. "Delft Services." *The Magazine Antiques*, December 1982.

Wynter, Harriet. *An Introduction to European Porcelain*. New York: 1972.

Appendix I
Value Ranges for Eighteenth Century Blue and White Porcelain

Sometime around the year 1690 an eight inch porcelain charger decorated in underglaze blue with the "Siege of Amsterdam" found its way from the kilns of the Far East to the bustling city of Delft in Holland. There, it was acquired at auction together with a few other pieces of blue and white porcelain by Count Vizthum in 1723 and finally came to the possession of King August the Strong. Once part of the Royal Collection it was catalogued and assigned the Johanneum number N: 414. Centuries later, in 2005, the charger (still in mint condition) came under the hammer once again, this time in Rochester, New York, where it fetched $3,300. This true story underscores the fact that a determined and well-informed collector can still obtain museum quality porcelain at affordable prices.

Throughout the book price ranges for many items were given in the figure captions. For understandable reasons no values were quoted for items currently in museums or private collections identified by name. Instead we have chosen to survey the auction records and quote prices for what was judged to be "museum" or "investment" quality porcelain. While it is safe to assume that such objects will command sustained collector interest, auction prices will always depend on economic conditions at the time of the sale and on how well the sale was advertised. That statement is also true for the price ranges quoted in the figure captions. All values are given for objects in very good to excellent condition unless noted otherwise.

A Meissen plate (8.75" in diameter) from c. 1730-35 decorated with crayfish in a manner similar to that shown in Fig. 110 was sold for approximately $6,000 (original auction outcomes were archived in Euros and have been converted to USD by the author using the exchange rate at the time of the writing). A Meissen covered sugar bowl from the same period (1732-35) and decorated in the pattern we have called Japanese Garden with Table (or *Tischchenmuster* cf. Figs. 114 and 332-341) realized $3,750. A Meissen tea bowl and saucer from 1720-30 decorated with gold Chinamen in the workshop of Bartholomäus Seuter of Augsburg (similar to Fig. 150) realized $2,500. Similarly a Meissen tea bowl and saucer from 1740-50 in the Rock and Bird Pattern with the underglaze blue decoration completely covered with gold (like in Figs. 152 and 153) brought $1,250. The reader should contrast these values to the prices for early eighteenth century polychrome decoration. A c. 1725-30 small covered jar (6.5" in diameter), decorated with elaborate chinoiserie by Höroldt, was sold for approx. $15,000. A 15" tall vase (Meissen) with plainer chinoiserie on bluish-green ground, ostensibly from the inventory of the Japanese Palace and bearing the AR (Augustus Rex) mark realized a final selling price in excess of $25,000.

Appendix II
Internet Resources

Several resources freely available on the Internet provide information complementary to many of the topics covered in this book. A degree of fluency in the German language is necessary to fully appreciate the content of some of the sites.

Wettiner History

The history of European porcelain is inextricably intertwined with the tastes, politics, and style of the Wettiner rulers of Saxony. Detailed information about Saxon history and the House of Wettin can be found in the following Internet sites.

http://www.die-sachsen-kommen.de/wetthtm/wettin.htm
http://www.haus-wettin.de

Père Francois Xavier d'Entrecolles

Père Francois Xavier d'Entrecolles (1664-1741) was a Jesuit missionary who traveled to China in 1698, where he observed some of the secrets of porcelain manufacture. His letters, written in 1712 and 1722, were among the first accounts available in the West on Chinese porcelain and helped to fuel the European craze for porcelain and the search for the "Arcanum", or the "secret" formula for porcelain. The letters have been translated from the French. The site presents the English version as it appears in William Burton's *Porcelain, It's Art and Manufacture*, B.T. Batsford, London, 1906. The web site has retained the original spelling, which may differ from the modern transliteration, e.g. "Ching-tê-chên" is today referred to as "Jingdezhen".

http://www.ceramicstoday.com/articles/entrecolles.htm

Virtual Museum Tours

Many of the museums that have contributed material to this book have informative web sites that offer virtual tours.

http://www.pem.org/homepage/
http://www.gardinermuseum.on.ca/default_flash.aspx
http://www.skd-dresden.de/de/museen/porzellansammlung/sammlung.html
http://www.duesseldorf.de/hetjens/
http://www.mkg-hamburg.de/

Manufacturer Sites

The reader may find the site of Dresden Porcelain, Inc., the former Carl Thieme factory, of considerable interest. It has a short movie showing the actual steps involved in the production of porcelain. The people in the movie are actually employees of the company filmed at work.

http://www.dresden-porcelain.com/default.htm

The Auction House Bergmann maintains a complete archive of the results realized at its own auctions, together with pictures and descriptions.

http://www.auction-bergmann.de/

Index of Persons

ORG IV.
AUGUST II.
AUGUST III.
FRI
1694 - 1733.
1733 - 1763.